YOUR DECK OF SUCCESS

Foreword by Dr. Michelle Mras

RICH PARSONS & DR. SMILEY

Jeremy McDonald • Julie Miller Davis • László Rém • Dr. Evi Abada • Felicia Masquat • Dr. Garrett Goggans
Dr. Jeannette Musset • Reverend Joanne Angel Barry Colon • Dr. KD Wagner • Dr. Debra Dean
Nancy Schwartz • Marc Perry • Kay McDonald • Craig Bruce • Teresa Rand • Dr. Patricia Boulogne
Gina Marie Lokken • Tracy Brown • Rosaline Gordon • Lea Hope Bonzer • Dr. Lamarr Renee Spencer
Sally Wurr • Margie Dunki-Jacobs • John Diggs • Cat Oshman • Michele Marshall • Seth Miller
Phyllis Caddell • Ken Lewis • David A. Aviles • Marcy Myles-Clark • Stephen Boyd • Nadia Hayes Simmons
Teresa Mack • Natalie McQueen • Heather Harris • Sharon Sills • Darryl Clack • Maggie Bellevue • Chad C. Betz
Diana "Dinky" Smith • Michael Wader • Dr. Rhonda Glover Reese • Dayna Caddell • Octavia E. Vance
Dawna Campbell • Wanda Muir Oliver • Vicki Wright-Hamilton • Pearl Chiarenza • Deidra Moore • Lisa Bischoff

Your Deck of Success, August 2023

ISBN: 978-1-64810-241-7

Printed in the United States of America

"If the cards are stacked against you,
reshuffle the deck."

- John C. MacDonald

"Life is like a game of cards.
The hand you are dealt is determinism;
the way you play it is free will."

-Jawaharlal Nehru

"Life is not always a matter of
holding good cards, but sometimes,
playing a poor hand well."

-Jack London

The four suits in playing cards, clubs, diamonds, hearts, and spades, collectively represent the four elements (wind, fire, water, and earth), the seasons and cardinal directions. They represent the struggle of opposing forces for victory in life. The thirteen cards in each suit represent the thirteen lunar months.

~ www.fleurdelis.com/symbols

Foreword

"Your life is not determined by the cards you are dealt, but by how you play them."
-Unknown

The stories within this book are condensed success lessons. Each author is an expert and professional in their fields. They share their unique success techniques with you. Although each is varied, there are three trends that come through: define success, take action, and surround yourself with positivity.

In the game to achieve success, it is important to define what success looks like to you. Much like fingerprints, success is unique to every individual. As such, how each person gets there will present itself differently.

Once you know what you are striving for, you must take action. If success was easy, everyone would have it. It is up to the individual to choose to put forth the effort necessary to achieve their idea of success. At times, the path may appear long and arduous. Remember that the journey of a thousand miles starts with a single step. Take that step.

To remain motivated during your journey, it's important to surround yourself with positive people and thoughts. Make a concerted effort to purge negativity and accentuate the positives in your life. If you do this, positive things will come to you.

You've already taken the first step toward success. You've chosen this book full of positive advice. Congratulations! Now, it's up to you to choose your definition of success. Find at least one story that resonates with you to be your guide and take strides toward your success.

The cards are at your disposal. Play your hand well. Go be the best version of you…Unapologetically.

Michelle Mras, PhD
January 2023

Prologue

Rich Parsons has his successful Colorado Springs based Your Success Magazine – to support and highlight entrepreneurs and small business owners. I am heavily involved in multiple endeavors: 1) Amplifluence is a traveling networking group which amplifies the notoriety of Speakers, Authors and Influencers in cities across the United States, 2) The KEEP SMILING MOVEMENT (501c3), and 3) My Perfect Publishing company. Since we met, Rich and I have supported each other in our various endeavors.

One day we were discussing how we could work together on a new level and the idea of this book was born. We began contacting experts highlighted in Rich's magazine to give them the opportunity to provide insight into what success means to them and how to achieve it.

Welcome to "Your Deck of Success"! Inside, you will find a collection of expert insights and practical advice from some of the most successful people across various industries. These individuals have excelled in their fields and have agreed to share their strategies and wisdom with you. You'll discover a wide range of success strategies, from setting goals and creating action plans, to developing leadership skills and building a strong personal brand. Whether you're an entrepreneur, a career professional, or someone looking to reach new heights in any area of your life, this anthology has something for you. Get ready to be inspired and motivated as you learn from the best and start developing your own success strategies.

The idea of a deck of cards came to mind because as there are fifty-two weeks in a year, there are that many cards in a deck. We found the idea profound to create playing cards for a Deck of Success where each author is represented by a card within the deck. Not only will the readers have the lessons within this book but can retrieve each author's success key from within the Deck of Success cards.

Dr. Smiley (Ken Rochon)

Table of Contents

Foreword vii

Prologue. ix

CLUBS 1

A♣ Rich Parsons 3

K♣ Jeremy McDonald 7

Q♣ Julie Miller Davis. 11

J♣ László Rém 15

10♣ Dr. Evi Abada 19

9♣ Felicia Masquat. 23

8♣ Dr. Garrett Goggans 27

7♣ Dr. Jeannette Musset. 31

6♣ Reverend Joanne Angel Barry Colon. 35

5♣ Dr. KD Wagner 39

4♣ Dr. Debra Dean 43

3♣ Nancy Schwartz 47

2♣ Marc Perry 53

HEARTS **57**

A♥ Kay McDonald. 59

K♥ Craig Bruce 65

Q♥ Teresa Rand. 69

J♥ Dr. Patricia Boulogne 73

10♥ Gina Marie Lokken. 79

9♥ Tracy Brown 85

8♥ Rosaline Gordon. 89

7♥ Lea Hope Bonzer 93

6♥ Dr. Lamarr Renee Spencer 97

5♥ Sally Wurr. 101

4♥ Margie Dunki-Jacobs 107

3♥ John Diggs 111

2♥ Cat Oshman. 115

SPADES **119**

A♠ Michele Marshall 121

K♠ Seth Miller 125

Q♠ Phyllis Caddell. 129

J♠ Ken Lewis 133

10♠ David A. Aviles 137

9♠ Marcy Myles-Clark 141

8♠ Stephen Boyd 145

7♠ Nadia Hayes Simmons 149

6♠ Teresa Mack. 153

5♠ Natalie McQueen 157
4♠ Heather Harris 161
3♠ Sharon Sills 165
2♠ Darryl Clack 169

DIAMONDS 173
A♦ Maggie Bellevue 175
K♦ Chad C. Betz 179
Q♦ Diana "Dinky" Smith 183
J♦ Michael Wader 187
10♦ Dr. Rhonda Glover Reese 191
9♦ Dayna Caddell 195
8♦ Octavia E. Vance 199
7♦ Dawna Campbell 203
6♦ Wanda Muir Oliver 207
5♦ Vicki Wright-Hamilton 211
4♦ Pearl Chiarenza 215
3♦ Deidra Moore 219
2♦ Lisa Bischoff 223

CLUBS

Otherwise known as trefoils, clubs represent many things: fall, winter, night, darkness, males, fire, energy, will, wealth, work, luck, and happiness.

~ www.fleurdelis.com/symbols

Ace of Clubs

A♣ Rich Parsons

A question I've had to ask myself at various points over the past several years is, "What is keeping me from achieving the success I want and the outcome I desire?" I imagine you have asked that same question, or similar, at various times as well. If you have not, I encourage you to take a little time to let that question settle within your mind and explore it further to answer it for yourself.

Success is such a popular word in many aspects of life and business. However, it's been my experience, personally and professionally, whether speaking with coaching clients or digging into it for my own good, that one of the top problems is that we do not have a good understanding of what success is. With that in mind, I would like to share a couple questions that I think will help you in your own exploration, just as it has in mine.

1) Have you <u>Defined Success</u> for what you are wanting to achieve?

I find that many times we are delayed in our success due to not actually defining what success looks like for the particular scenario. When we define it and shape some form of measurement, we are then able to better focus our efforts on what is going to create the desired outcome.

When you properly complete this step, you are then able to move forward in creating goals, objectives and action steps to start the process.

2) Have you Determined Why it is important to be successful?

The desire to be successful can be broken down through a series of simple questions, and telling responses, to get to the root of it all.

If you have ever completed a problem-solving exercise using the Ishikawa Diagram, named after Kaoru Ishikawa, you've basically walked out this exercise. You simply ask, "Why is [your response to previous question] important to you?" With each response getting closer to the deep-rooted cause.

One of the exercises I share with clients is a Defining Success Worksheet in which I have them answer seven or eight questions dealing with the definition/description of success, and a series of why/what questions. By the end of the exercise, they have defined success, how it is relevant to them and their goal, and ultimately how being successful will make them feel.

So, just as I would encourage coaching clients to complete this exercise, I encourage you to put in the work to define success for yourself. Drill down to find the ultimate why, then describe the feeling that success will bring to you. If you do this, I am confident that you will be able to achieve success in anything you put your mind, heart and effort to.

Here's to your success!

Rich Parsons is a Success Coach and the Founder of Your Success Magazine. He helps entrepreneurs and business professionals create success and use their message as part of their success strategy in personal and professional ventures. His primary focus is to provide space for others to share their message and business to a global audience.

King of Clubs

K♣ Jeremy McDonald

What is success? I've been thinking about this very thought. As I pondered what I was going to write, the answer that came to me is happiness and fulfillment. For me, if you feel fulfilled and you are happy with the direction your life is going, then you already are successful. The next question should be, "How do I get there?"

To put it simply, to be fulfilled, you must be working on something that feels like fulfillment. That could be many things from living healthier, achieving goals, having a loving family with a beautiful spouse and children, or a successful business or career. Whatever that looks like, is up to you.

Discover something you are passionate about and work towards that passion. Often, we hold ourselves back from taking a step forward because we get overwhelmed with how to achieve our goals. Just start somewhere! Start small. What I have learned is small, decisive steps eventually work into big things, but nothing happens if you do nothing.

As you take those small steps, it will be natural for you to get frustrated, to judge yourself, or even want to give up; but don't give up. Take a break if you need one but get back to it and keep pushing forward. Perseverance, practice, and a constant drive to learn, is what is going to help you grow into your dreams.

Just remember that successful people are not born; they are developed over time. Even the ones that appear they were handed a silver spoon had things they worked on to achieve their goals. So, be kind to yourself and allow yourself to make mistakes, to get discouraged, and to even fail. The important thing is for you to get back up and try again!

I will leave you with this. I have dyslexia. I was told all my life by my peers and even some teachers, that there are certain things I would not be able to do. However, I am living proof that you can do anything you set your mind to. Sure, you may take longer than others and you may need to get additional education. But if you want it bad enough, then you will achieve it. My learning disability is not my disadvantage; it is the foundation of my success because it gave me something to overcome and to grow from. All of you have that same ability. Now go out and live your life and be happy!

Jeremy McDonald is an International Best-Selling Author and Speaker with over 25 years of experience as a public speaker & coach. Jeremy brings his diverse range of experience to help people reach their highest potential. Jeremy is the show host at The Los Angeles Tribune's Roku TV network and the organizer of the Spirit Heart Cruise.

Queen of Clubs

Q♣ Julie Miller Davis

In the 8 years that JMD Productivity has been in existence, and in the 14 years I've been an entrepreneur, I have found that the number one reason business owners get stuck is time. They don't have time to get the important things done; they are treating all things equally and thus not prioritizing and wasting time. They don't have time to implement big ideas they know would grow their businesses. They don't have time to take on more or bigger clients without sacrificing even more time. Sound familiar?

Most often, when people think they have a time management issue, they actually have a calendar and task list issue. The truth is, until you manage that monster of a task list, you'll be stuck in a vortex of slow or non-growth for a long time.

So, in order to open up space and create time, you need to start with that list. If you can get it prioritized and pared down to a manageable size, you'll be on the right track. Where I start with most of my clients and audiences is using my "3 D's system". You must decide what you need to DO, what you can

DELEGATE, and what you can DUMP. To get started, ask yourself these questions:

1. Is this something that **only I** can do? These are the **DO** its on your list.
2. Is this something that someone else could do 80% of? Or is this something that if someone did it 80% as well as I can, would that be good enough? If the answer is yes to either of these, they are your **DELEGATE** items.
3. Is this something that could be done later or that doesn't really need to be done at all? Both of these are **DUMP** items.

Once you have designated a "D" to an item, it's important then to either put it on the calendar, put it in someone else's hands or to take it off the list completely.

The system goes a lot further than outlined here. The next step is the actual prioritization of the things on the list and then the interfacing with your calendar. But if nothing else, this should get you started on your road to mastering that task list and making more time for the things that matter in your business. Go out, Do, Delegate, and Dump, and be productive!

A driven entrepreneur serving others by helping them reach their goals, **Julie Miller Davis** works with business owners and leaders to reset their productivity patterns, become more efficient, and bust through roadblocks to reach their goals with excellence. An award-winning coach and trainer, Julie has led and developed highly successful teams, helped hundreds escalate their own businesses and achieve goals they may never have thought possible. Even in the year of the pandemic, many of Julie's clients under her watch broke 6 figures for the first time! Her superpower of out-of-the-box thinking uncovers new ways to solve business stagnation, resulting in growth and propelling her clients into new and exciting directions.

Jack of Clubs

J♣ László Rém

Success is a State of Being and Feeling!

"I can't do it, but I have to, even if it kills me!"
"Permanence is death; I have to keep moving."

Do these sound familiar?

Understanding. To achieve this state of being, your mind is *"helping you"* create things, but only based on your previous experiences. For example, when you think you have to "*sacrifice something to achieve something*", there is a place for this thought in your environment. Your thoughts, feelings, and habits (beliefs) match this idea. "*Are there people who have succeeded in their lives, but did not sacrifice as much as you?*" After you've asked yourself this question, pay attention to your thoughts and feelings! **Metaphysics** is a branch of philosophy that deals with the nature of reality and the relationship between mind and matter. We are talking about how thoughts and feelings manifest into reality. When you think about doing something, your mind can walk you through the steps to do that by choosing from stored experiences, and it will "tell you" what is possible. Or, conversely, it puts forth every effort to make you avoid certain actions. Your feelings also act the same way, either supporting or limiting you. This is your **Inner Communication.** The only reason your mind and feelings do this is to keep your body and yourself safe! If something feels good, you will feel comfortable around it, even if you know it isn't the best for you. *"I don't have time for living healthy!"* And if it feels bad, you consider that thing uncomfortable, even if it's something others would find pleasing. "*Vacation? Are you out of your mind?*"

Observing. Simply being in the current moment without passing judgment on it lowers stress and enhances concentration and ***decision-creating***. Begin to pay attention to your thoughts, feelings, breathing, the rustling of the leaves, or the sounds of rain on the window. Any judgments you form are influenced by your prior experiences. But if you quiet your mind and feelings, you can create new steps that will elicit a range of new emotions and fresh thoughts. By paying attention to your thoughts and feelings, you move from reacting to creating.

Creating. After you understand the history and this strong dualistic approach to your actions and feelings, you are ready to change. By asking yourself, "***This is what I want in my life! What can I do to shift and change, to gain or have this?***", you just set your intention to experience new things.

Being and feeling successful is a path. Know and adjust (if needed) what you want to achieve! It's possible to know and feel what's right for you and your community.

László Rém, a former architect, is now assisting people with a fusion of Western knowledge and Eastern ideas, in remembering who they are and living happy and fulfilled lives. He blends his engineering side with a love of inspiring others to achieve success in their personal and professional lives.

Ten of Clubs

10♣ Dr. Evi Abada

Deliberate Actions for Success

Success is a relative term and means different things to different people. For simplicity, according to the Merriam-Webster dictionary, "Success is a favorable or desired outcome." As individuals, our desired outcomes can be different, and to become successful, we have the unique responsibility of defining what those outcomes are. As a physician, I have had to define my desired outcome at different professional career stages. Fundamentally, success is not accidental but involves a conscious and deliberate set of tasks geared toward achieving the desired outcome. Becoming successful requires intentionality. It requires us to be active, not passive in our decisions or actions.

A great place to start our success journeys is **defining what success means** for the individual. What does success mean to you? And what are the parameters to measure that degree of success? I define success by setting goals that are invariably tied to my desired outcome. That way, I can measure my progress, change strategies if necessary, and work with a set of timelines. Of course, setting goals that are SMART (Specific, Measurable, Achievable, Relevant, and Time-bound) is the standard.

In achieving our definition of success, we must give room for **flexibility**. There are times when things may not go as planned and being flexible enough to change the strategy, but not the goal, is very important for achieving success. Therefore, having a clear definition of what success means from the beginning for the individual is very important. As we adapt to the changes and nuances that we might encounter during the journey toward success, we must never lose sight of the goal.

While certain ventures in life may be driven by speed, **consistency** is the driving force for success. Learning to go bit by bit and taking one step at a time towards the goal is paramount to becoming successful. This approach not only prevents burnout, but also ensures that we are active participants in ensuring that our physical, mental, emotional, and spiritual health are all intact while we pursue our goals of becoming successful.

Furthermore, as we navigate the path toward success, we must be prepared to **step outside our comfort zones** and reach out for opportunities that may not present themselves or become available to us if we get too familiar with our cozy little cocoons.

Becoming successful requires intentionality, grit, and familiarity with the dynamics of time and the resources available to you. Additionally, being open and flexible enough to adapt based on your unique circumstance is key to achieving success.

Dr. Evi Abada is a Diplomate of the American Board of Pathology. She served as Chief Resident during her residency training and is the 2022/2023 Chair of the Resident Council of the American Society for Clinical Pathology. Dr. Abada is a passionate writer and regularly writes to inspire her readers. When she is not working, Dr. Abada loves to spend time with her family. Connect with Dr. Abada or LinkedIn @EviAbadaMDMS or Twitter @EviAbadaMD

Nine of Clubs

9♣ Felicia Masquat

Goal Setting Starts with a List: From my experience, writing down my goals has been a game changer. Grab a piece of paper and just start writing down your goals. Write whatever comes to mind. You can go through your list and organize it. Set a few realistic goals to achieve with a deadline. Get creative with how you layout your goals. Whether you use paper, a vision board, or a computer. Make it stand out to be a visual reminder of what needs to be accomplished. It is a great idea to revisit your goals and rethink your strategies to achieve them.

Practicing a Positive Mindset: It's important to think and speak kindly to yourself. I understand at times, negative thoughts of self-doubt pop in, "I can't do it. It's too difficult." I am guilty of having those types of thoughts in the past. You can rewire those negative thoughts with positive ones. Choose one affirmation to counter a negative thought you wish to work on. Write down the affirmations ten times daily in the morning and/or night. Speak the affirmation aloud until that thought is reversed. A few affirmations I use are: "I have power over my own life", "I am bright, brilliant, and beautiful." Repeat as needed and watch the positive thoughts flow effortlessly.

Your Circle is an Important Part of Your Success: Surround yourself with individuals that inspire and motivate you; someone you want to be like. Most high-level successful individuals are willing to share their knowledge with you. If you have an opportunity to ask an individual to be your mentor, then go for it. Having someone to ask questions on their career success, provide guidance, knowledge, motivation, and moral support. You could go as far as having two mentors. One female and one male to get a diverse perspective. Also, attending networking meetings, conferences, and speaking events will give you a chance to meet those types of individuals you need in your circle.

Manifesting means to create something or turn something from an idea into a reality. Create a dream board with pictures, colors, stickers, and anything that is a great visual for you. By visualizing it, writing it, speaking it, and believing in yourself, you will manifest your success.

Believe it! Write it! Speak it! Visualize it! Repeat!

Felicia Masquat, a single mother of four, a Health Promotions Educational Director, Inspirationalist, and Life Coach. She holds her Bachelor of Science Degree in Management and is an enrolled member in the Winnebago Tribe of Nebraska. Felicia has felt called to serve women in their thirties that have or are currently walking through the fires of life. Felicia is a survivor of abusive relationships, alcohol abuse, substance abuse, and has gone through divorce and the challenges of being a single mom. She uses her own life experiences to help women realize they are not alone in their struggles, nor do they have to do life alone. Felicia's biggest gift is connection, which you feel when she shares her inspiration for a brighter side of life.

Eight of Clubs

8♣ Dr. Garrett Goggans

The Boundaries of Belief

If I could provide what I consider to be the one tool that can make or break your success, it would be your belief. Some might question my distinction that belief is a tool. Our belief system is just something that we have, but it is that "belief" that actually proves my point. The idea that our beliefs are what they are and cannot be changed comes with a fixed mindset. A growth mindset will understand that our beliefs will set the bar on what we can achieve in life. So, if we want to raise the bar, we are going to have to change our beliefs about it.

I love to watch the expressions of people when I tell them that their beliefs are not their own, followed by the aha moment as I explain what that means. Our belief system, at its core, came from what was passed down to us from those that we love and trust. The Greek philosopher Aristotle once said, "Give me a child until he is seven and I will show you the man." What he meant by this is that our foundational belief systems are nurtured into us by those who took part in raising us. As we get older, we will begin to buy into the beliefs of others who present a good enough argument for us not to question it and run. So, it truly is the beliefs of others that we are walking around with and whatever we believe to be true, will be.

Whatever we hold in our belief system, our subconscious will seek to prove it as true. If you believe that you cannot achieve something, your subconscious will show you every reason why you should not try. It is our belief of who we are that is setting the limits of what we can and cannot achieve. I would encourage you to challenge those beliefs. Understand that people have accomplished so many things that went against what they were taught because they refused to believe they had limitations. The beauty of beliefs is that they are not who we are.

Beliefs are simply programs that our subconscious uses to analyze the thoughts we are inputting into it to determine the programmed output. If you do not like the current output simply change the program. Think of all the times you changed your belief because something caused you to reevaluate it. Once your belief changed, your behaviors around it changed. In this case the program, your belief, becomes the tool. If that belief is not serving your purpose, change it to one that will.

Dr. W. Garrett Goggans is an Author, Speaker, and Mindset Coach. Through positivity, encouragement, and an overwhelming sense of faith, he has helped others look past their current situations and find success in any endeavor. Dr. Goggans provides the roadmap to hit goals most never thought were achievable through a proven 12-step framework he calls the Mindset Engineering System and further offers encouragement through his writings and podcast show called *Moving Upstream Without a Paddle*.

Seven of Clubs

7♣ Dr. Jeannette Musset

In the world we live in today, I know that many patients are tired of "quick fixes." They seek a more natural approach to their health and a doctor that considers their medical and cultural background.

As a Naturopathic Physician and owner of a Naturopathic practice based in Scottsdale, AZ, we offer high-level medical care, cutting-edge therapies, and advanced technology to a diverse group of patients. More specifically, we provide our patients natural therapies to address hormone imbalances, skin concerns, unexplained weight gain, and loss of sex drive. With my global perspective, I can tailor treatments that consider our patient's culture and beliefs. I've discovered that providing personalized holistic treatment to my patients has empowered them to take control of their health. I have over 11 years of experience working with conventional medicine. This experience, paired with my knowledge of Naturopathic medicine, allows me to provide natural health options that merge holistic and conventional medicine together.

My message to all entrepreneurs and what I thrive to do in my own life is, "Your business success starts with your health." If you want to make massive wealth, your health must be a priority. When business owners have low energy, are sleep deprived, too stressed, gaining weight, have bedroom issues, or hair loss concerns, it reflects on the way they show up for their success, their leadership skills, and their confidence.

My goal is to take their health to the next level so they can feel even more rejuvenated, have more stamina, improved brain performance, less sick time off, and win in the bedroom, so they can focus on what they do best. Investing in your health as a business professional will help you be more even, more productive, efficient, and, in the long run, be more profitable.

Modern medicine should now be geared towards prevention and taking into considerations lifestyle changes rather than just looking at the symptoms. Food is medicine, exercise is anti-aging, the best pill for stress is meditation. Is your doctor talking to you about these treatments? This is healthcare that puts you in control of your own health and not the doctor or the insurance company. I believe this approach and this type of medicine holds the key to success and to achieve total health for all business professionals.

Dr. Jeannette Musset is a Naturopathic Physician and Founder of Healthcierge Medical. Her team empowers individuals to elevate their health and wellness. She is in business to provide superior patient care and strongly believes that everyone should spend more time with their doctors and get high quality personalized care.

Six of Clubs

6♣ Reverend Joanne Angel Barry Colon

I rely on Astrology and Numerology to help me activate success. Each day of the week is associated with a specific planet and theme.

Mondays are ruled by the Moon, a day for stepping into our emotions, intuition, and true potential. Mondays help us get clear about the project, contracts, and partnerships we want to accomplish for that week. The Moon is the ruler of Cancer, which helps strengthen our intuition, instincts, and habits.

Tuesdays are ruled by Mars, a day for action, moving forward on projects, getting things done, and being passionate about our goals, dreams, and desires. Mars is the ruler of Aries, which helps us be a warrior and a leader.

Wednesdays are ruled by Mercury, a day of communication, expression, creativity, group meetings, and events. Mercury is the ruler of Gemini, which helps us to communicate and schedule time for meetings, marketing, brainstorming, and all things related to social media.

Thursdays are ruled by Jupiter, a day of expansion, gifts, and a perfect day for everything to come together. Jupiter is the ruler of Sagittarius, which helps us work with our intuition and creative side of the brain and travel for big business meetings, activate luck, abundance, and success.

Fridays are ruled by Venus, a day for business relationships, handling money, signing contracts, and connections. Venus is the ruler of Taurus, which helps us be more conscious of our physical and material possessions, business relationships, and monetary transactions.

Saturdays are ruled by Saturn, a day of organization and taking responsibility and also a great day to get balanced and grounded. Saturn is the ruler of Capricorn, which helps us activate our Soul's Purpose, recognize our accomplishments, and prepares us to take action for the week ahead.

Sundays are ruled by the Sun, a day of rest, unwinding, and connecting with our inner self. Sun is the ruler of Leo, which helps us reflect on spiritual growth, self-expression and our creativity while reminding us that work must be fun and having freedom is success.

The New Moon is a great time to activate New Business and the Full Moon is a great time to let go of partnerships, contracts, and projects that no longer serve you.

Reverend Joanne Angel Barry Colon has 35+ years in the health, fitness, and wellness industry and 15+ years in the Healing industry. She is the Founder of Wholistic Fitness, Certified Wholistic Personal Trainer, Intuitive Healer, Cosmic Energy Reader, Medical Astrologer, Master of Numerology, Host of Joanne's Healing Within T.V. Show and Joanne's Cosmic Energy Radio Show, Author/Self-Publisher and the Creator of Chakra Balance Numerology Cosmic Energy Forecast Deck. Joanne has helped, educated and healed over 20,000 women (and men by referral). She helps release issues from their tissues as they release emotional weight and fall in love with themselves.

Five of Clubs

5♣ Dr. KD Wagner

Don't Get Lost in the Loss

Have you or someone you know experienced a loss? A loss of a loved one, relationship, career, or pet? Did that loss result in depression, or even suicidal feelings?

You might be asking yourself, "What does Dr. KD know about loss and pain?"

On March 26, 2001, my eighteen-year-old son, Jeffrey, was murdered by gun violence.

On August 28, 2003, my twenty-four-year-old son, Bud, was murdered in a felony hit and run.

These two days changed my life forever. My world turned upside down and inside out. Everything I had lived and worked for was GONE. I barely hung on by my fingernails to my sanity. I swirled into a hurricane of emotions as I struggled to find any reason to stay on Earth.

Suffering from Complicated Grief and Post Traumatic Stress Disorder (PTSD), death would not stop. I also lost eight other close family members in the same nine-year period. Lost in the depths of hell, I survived moment to moment. I went to bed and woke up playing "*would have, could have, should have*" games in my head.

Do these kinds of thoughts keep you up at night? I know they kept me up. Wouldn't it be nice to make the games in your head stop? Even in a room full of people, I felt alone.

Nobody should ever be in the depths of hell, left behind, and alone. Thankfully, I stumbled upon three secrets that saved my life.

1. I stopped questioning everything.
   a. No more "*would have, could have, should have*" games.

2. I found a new purpose.
   a. I fulfilled a promise to my sons and earned two college degrees to honor them.
   b. I wrote *The Next Day Came Trilogy* so my sons will never be forgotten as I shared the stories of *Jeffrey—The Injustice of Murder, Bud—Homicide Turns a Blue Star Gold,* and *Kathy—How I Survived Tragic Loss*, along with *The Next Day Came Trilogy Thoughts and Emotions Activity Book* to help people explore their emotions and feelings.
   c. I became an International Best-Selling Author, and International Public Speaker, honoring my sons.

3. I joined a community of like-minded mothers.
    a. After the loss of Bud in the U.S. Navy, I became a Gold Star Mother and joined their National Organization—American Gold Star Mothers, Inc. Together, we help each other heal and honor our children by supporting veterans, their families, and the community.

These three steps led to the creation of *The Limitless Resilience System*, a solution that changed everything. These secrets could also help you, or a person you know.

For over twenty-one years I have shown others who suffered a loss, and are ready to move forward, how to stop the insanity, find limitless resilience, a new purpose, and learn to live a joyful life again.

What would it be worth to learn the secrets that I discovered, in a faster, simpler way?

The Limitless Resilience System achieves faster results, changes lives, and is priceless.

Are you ready to live a joyful life again? Find more information at: AGoldStarMom.com

Dr. KD Wagner is a multiple bestselling author, EIPPY Award winner, international speaker, and former law enforcement officer. Through *The Next Day Came trilogy,* Wagner shares her journey through loss, grief, depression, addiction, planned suicide, and survival after the loss of her two sons in separate homicides. KD has appeared on NBC, ABC, CBS, FOX, and stages with Joint Chief of Staff General Mark Milley, Governor/ Senator Rick Scott, country singer Rockie Lynne, and Bob Circosta, CEO and Founder of the Home Shopping Network. A Gold Star Mother—whose son died while serving in the U.S. Navy—KD serves as the President of the Florida Gulf Coast Chapter within the American Gold Star Mothers, Inc.

Four of Clubs

4♣ Dr. Debra Dean

I attribute my success to being hard-working, hard-headed and not giving up. I am passionate about helping people. I love to see them stretch to do more than they thought they ever could. I have a natural gift to see the good in people and to see potential in every single human being on the planet. I love people.

My three keys for living a life of success are:

(a) Define success and what it looks like for you.
(a) Like any organization would, establish a strategic plan to succeed.
(a) Recruit the right people for your team.

Define Success: I used to think success was the big title, cozy corner office with an awesome view, and large amounts of money. Now, I define success as living a life without compromise for Christ. All of the material things of this world will not matter when we die. Therefore, the most important decision that any of us can make is whether we are going to heaven or hell when we die. Trusting in the Lord Jesus Christ is the most important decision we can make. From there, all other things fall into place as we put God first and treat people the way we want to be treated. What does success look like for you? If you were to die today, what would people say at your funeral about how you lived your life and what legacy would you leave? What are you willing to compromise on today that may or may not honor and please God? Are your values in line with the values of the Bible or with the values of the world?

Strategic Plan: Living a life to honor and glorify God looks radically different from living a life of worldly success. Lay out your 5 or 10-year plan with milestones of what you want to accomplish. Do you want to be debt free? Dave Ramsey says, "If you will live like no one else, later you can live like no one else." When you are debt free, you can do things with your money like paying for a stranger's coffee or giving away money to your favorite charity. Establish your strategic plan by thinking about what you want people to remember about you or what you would be proud of if you caught people having a conversation about you behind your back. For me, I want more of God and less of me. I want to spend every day of my life honoring and glorifying God in all that I do. Consider the future and align your daily living with the strategic plan of your life.

Recruit Your Team: When asked how I could work full time; earn a Bachelor, Master, and Doctoral degree; and raise a family all at the same time, I attribute perseverance, hard work, follow-through, and boundaries as keys to success. It is imperative that we have a team around us to succeed. Boundaries are necessary to move people into their strategic positions, like on a chessboard. I could not have naysayers holding me back.

Instead, I needed my inner circle to be full of cheerleaders and people that truly supported my mission and me, or, at the very least, did not act as an obstacle to success. I needed people that would challenge me and stretch my thinking. I also needed people around me to pray for me. Every successful organization has a board of directors – you should too. Whom will you select to be on your team?

As you consider these three keys to living a life of success, I want to also encourage you to take action today. All too often, we put off our own needs due to work or family obligations. I am giving you permission to take care of yourself. Today, start to define what success means for you.

I challenge you to shift your mindset and daily decisions to those things that will honor and please God more than patting ourselves on the back for an earthly job well done.

If I can be of assistance, please reach out to drdebra@drdebradean.com.

Dr. Debra J. Dean is co-founder of His Kingdom Matters, a ministry designed to encourage and equip Christians to live in the world, but not of the world. She uses her 25 years of corporate experience and Ph.D. in Organizational Leadership from one of the top conservative Christian schools in the country to turn eyes to Jesus and inspire an awakening of moral consciousness and holy living in the United States. Dr. Dean has lived a life full of hard knocks, but by some standards, she is a success. She is married, has six children, and six grandchildren, and has accomplished titles such as Miss Teen USA, Woman of Influence, and Operational Excellence Leader of the Year. She climbed the corporate ladder to earn six figures and have a respectable title. She also earned a black belt in Tae Kwon Do and finished the Triple Crown of Running. Despite worldly titles, Dr. Dean explains that her definition of success changed from material worth to eternal decisions.

Three of Clubs

3♣ Nancy Schwartz

YOU Planning™

When I retired, I searched for that course or book to propel me into the next phase of my life. Unfortunately, most of the retirement advice is focused on the financial aspect of planning and encourages us to start early. Time should be on your side, counsels the experts. That's terrific and bravo to you if you followed that advice to capture the markets and feel more or less secure in your financial retirement. What they don't tell you, and frankly it's never discussed, is that YOU are the most important piece of the retirement equation. Your health isn't discussed either. Isn't that a key part in how you will enjoy your future decades? The average American is 88% metabolically unfit, and to top that, the World Health Organization says that most people spend the last 16 years of their life in poor health.

Retirement is a life experience, something you can't fully imagine until you live it day after day. It's similar to your first job, marriage, or getting that promotion – it stands alone in the category of life's milestones. What I understood over the next several years of educating myself from top global experts in health and retirement, was there was no communication around the retirement transformation. That's why I wrote an educational tool to support you, called YOU Planning™.

Success Hack #1: YOU PLAN

We are a society that plans for everything, except we don't plan for ourselves in retirement. Additionally, longevity and quality of aging are now coming into play. In today's world, quality of life and health span need to be included in the definition of lifestyle.

A question to ask:

Who are you becoming as you move from a career into healthy retirement?

This isn't a selfish question, rather it is time for self-reflection, expansion and defining your new WHY.

Takeaway #1:

Put yourself first for the first time in your life.

Success Hack # 2: OWN YOU

Owning all of you is an important step for your agency. In our careers, we sought outgrowth opportunities. Other areas in our life lacked that attention because of time or focus. This may be around the categories of physical, spiritual, relationships, emotions, a new career in retirement, finances, philanthropy, or something else that matters dearly to you.

A question to ask:

What areas in your life, outside of your career, may need further support? Cultivate it and think through the lens of life's long game. Many of the above categories you will find are interwoven.

Takeaway #2:

Live life with integrity, meaning your words matter, but it is your actions that count the most.

Success Hack #3: MOVE YOU

The CDC announced, "Only half of all US adults get the exercise they need. Approximately, 50% of the entire population lives with chronic illness, half of them suffer from two conditions or more."

Most people are allergic to movement. It isn't that you have had a sporadic relationship to movement, it's simply that this relationship is an accumulation of decades of unmet physical activity. Life gets in the way.

A question to ask:

How can I start to move consistently?

Takeaway #3:

Start with continual movement throughout your day. Movement improves heart rate variability and increases lung capacity. It also builds muscle mass, especially needed in shaping your longevity.

As I thought about a healthy retirement, these science-based success hacks from the educational tool YOU Planning™ guided me. My hope for you is that they will support your healthy retirement transformation as well.

Nancy Schwartz is the Founder and Transformational Strategist of Envision Healthy Retirement. Today, Nancy works with business experts focusing on the client's science-based transformation from a career into a healthy retirement. Formerly, she was partner in a global management consulting company. Her innovative and solution-oriented approach to solving complex problems earned her high praise and recognition. Nancy graduated from Skidmore College and was a professional dancer. Additionally, she is a member of select mentorships in both health and business.

Two of Clubs

2♣ Marc Perry

Success Leaves Clues

In my journey through life and my career, two fundamental principles imparted to me by two incredible individuals have become the guiding beacons of my success. The first, instilled in me by my beloved father, Lawrence C. Perry, was the timeless adage, "Plan your work and work your plan." The second, bestowed upon me by my esteemed mentor, Donald S. Vest, Sr., resonated deeply within me, "Inspect what you expect." These two principles have not only shaped my professional trajectory but have also become foundational elements that have paved the way for my achievements.

My dad, Lawrence, was a man of profound wisdom and unparalleled work ethic. He always emphasized the significance of having a well-thought-out plan and the dedication to execute it meticulously. From an early age, I remember him sitting with me at the kitchen table, teaching me the art of planning. He taught me that without a clear direction and a comprehensive roadmap, success would remain elusive. I embraced this invaluable advice, realizing that goals without a plan are mere dreams and dreams without a plan are nightmares. So, in every venture, whether personal or professional, I made it a habit to strategize meticulously, setting measurable milestones that would lead me closer to my objectives.

A lifelong friend of my father who became my mentor, Donald S. Vest, Sr., is a seasoned professional with a wealth of experience, who epitomizes a strong leader. Donald emphasized that setting expectations was essential but equally vital was to inspect and monitor progress. "Inspect what you expect" became my mantra, fueling my approach to leadership and management. Through his guidance, I understood that accountability was a vital component of success, not only for oneself but also for those under my guidance. I embraced this principle, and it significantly enhanced my ability to assess performance, identify potential roadblocks, and implement necessary course corrections.

Over the years, I combined the wisdom of both my father and my mentor. I learned to craft robust plans that aligned with the organization's vision while breaking them down into actionable steps. Additionally, the principle of "inspecting what we expect" became an integral part of my leadership style. I fostered an environment where open communication and feedback were encouraged, understanding that honest assessments were the bedrock of growth and improvement.

As I reflect on my journey, I credit these two principles gifted to me by Lawrence C. Perry and Donald S. Vest, Sr., for the successes I've achieved in my career. Their wisdom remains ingrained in my heart and mind, a constant reminder that strategic planning and diligent execution, coupled with vigilant monitoring and accountability, form the cornerstones of prosperity. I will forever be grateful for the invaluable life lessons bestowed upon me by these exceptional individuals, which have molded me into the professional I am today. Indeed, as I look back, I can clearly see that success leaves clues.

Marc Perry, an innovative leader and Goldman Sachs 10kSB scholar, heads Advantage Communications, a 20-year-old NMSDC minority-owned certified marketing agency. With a proven track record in multicultural marketing, our agency fosters diversity, equity, and inclusion.

HEARTS

Hearts represent the warmth of spring and summer seasons and the power of light. They are the center of life and the world. In the Tarot, hearts can also symbolize knowledge, love, life from water, and fertility, and in fortune-telling, joy.

~ www.fleurdelis.com/symbols

Ace of Hearts

A♥ Kay McDonald

Blending Passion and Purpose:
KEYS to SUCCESS for Businesses

Did you know that 85% of consumers prefer to do business with a business that gives back?

It's just GOOD BUSINESS to do GOOD. Adding a charity aspect to your business model can give it added purpose and direction. Charity partnerships can engage your team, show your clients you care, and provide a philanthropic story that is a win/win for both you and the charity(s) you choose to support.

3 MODELS TO CONSIDER:

1) PURPOSE DRIVEN BUSINESS: "Profit isn't a purpose; It's a result. To have purpose means the things we do are of real value to others." ~Simon Sinek

Purpose-driven companies attract the best minds, have the most passionate customers, achieve wild success and change the world. When purpose and passion are combined, the impact is powerful not only for individuals, but also on the public they serve to help create a brighter future for everyone.

2) CORPORATE SOCIAL RESPONSIBILITY: "Corporate social responsibility (CSR) is a term used to describe a company's efforts to improve society in some way. These efforts can range from donating money to nonprofits to implementing environmentally friendly policies in the workplace." -Double the Donation

CSR impacts companies, nonprofits, and employees alike. Corporate social responsibility is not a mandated practice in the United States; instead, it is something extra that companies do to improve their local and global communities.

3) SOCIAL ENTERPRISE: "Organizations that address a basic unmet need or solve a social or environmental problem through a market-driven approach" -Social Enterprise Network. Examples of market-driven approaches include:

Opportunity Employment: Organizations that employ people who have significant barriers to mainstream employment. Examples include Goodwill Industries, Greyston Bakery and Nisolo.

Transformative Products or Services: Organizations that create social or environmental impact through innovative products and services. Examples include Benetech, Growing Sound and Soles4Souls.

Donate Back: organizations that contribute a portion of their profits to nonprofits that address basic unmet needs. Examples include Everly, The Thx Co. and Songs Against Slavery.

Your business may be one or a combination of the examples above. Regardless, you should be integrating some aspect of doing good, because it's the right thing to do, and because people have big hearts.

HOW TO FIND THE RIGHT CAUSE FOR YOUR COMPANY

This is your chance to create social impact with meaning, and the right choice will fuel your soul and benefit your business. There are three things to consider when selecting:

1) What cause are you passionate about? You want to choose one(s) that you and your employees will embrace.

2) Does the charity need more of your time or your money? If you have lots of time and hands, choose an organization that needs volunteers. If you are a busy business owner, you may want to focus on how you can contribute financially to limit your time commitment and maximize your impact.

3) Does the cause align with your business? Try to find a nonprofit that has a mission that aligns with your business, for example: A restaurant business could align with a food bank. Pet food businesses can align with an animal rescue organization. Hair Salons might align with a women's cancer

organization. A real estate company could support a homeless shelter.

There are over 1,800,000 non-profits in the USA so there will be no shortage for you to choose from. You can research what charities might interest you by simply doing a Google search by cause.

CAUSE MARKETING and how it can work for you:

Now that you have chosen your cause and identified the best method and resources your company can use to support them, it's time to let the world know. When a business and charity align for the common purpose of profit and awareness it's called CAUSE MARKETING, and this can be a fresh new angle for your company to create content.

Aligning with a cause can provide a tangible contribution with BIG impact for the charity. Create a unique philanthropic story for social media to engage clients and employees to support your philanthropy.

"Spread the word, spread awareness,
feel GOOD about doing GOOD."
~ Kay McDonald

BRAINSTORM with Me. My business, Charity Charms is a purpose driven social enterprise that provides a vehicle to align companies with causes. I have been in the industry 20 years and enjoy connecting with cause minded e*ntities.*

Kay McDonald is the founder of Charity Charms, LLC and a bestselling author of two books (The Power of Charms and Awakening the Amazing in You). She believes in combining passion with purpose to achieve a life of success. Her main business, Charity Charms is a combination of Fashion and Compassion, which since 2004, has supported over 500 organizations worldwide with a tangible way to engage their communities through the Power of Charms.

King of Hearts

K♥ Craig Bruce

Ignite You and Play Your Best Hand Now: Three Game Changers to Get Even More from Your Life

Do you own YOU the way you own the boardroom?

In today's fast-paced world, many of us feel the stress of maintaining a busy and often chaotic lifestyle. This overwhelming sense of "lifestyle fatigue" can have a negative impact on our health, relationships and career.

After years of living this chaotic lifestyle, I finally learned that prioritizing YOU is what ultimately determines the level of success in your career and personal relationships. YOU are the common denominator in all of your life experiences.

Doesn't it make sense to invest time in YOU?

After retiring from a high-pressure career in Management Consulting, I began a journey researching science-based solutions for the mind and body.

I discovered that anyone can get even more from their life without sacrificing their career and key relationships. Through coaching hundreds of high-performing business leaders and entrepreneurs, I found three key areas that are game changers for empowering leaders to even more success. These key areas are:

- Mindset
- Lifestyle
- Community

Mindset is who you are being and how you show up every day. It involves growth, clarity and intention. It is about identifying your top values and non-negotiables and using them as filters for all your decisions. Values like your health, partner, spouse, kids, grandkids or career.

Lifestyle is how you live your life to support your mind and body for longevity. Focusing on how you nourish, restore (sleep!) and move your body are key components to IGNITE YOU. Build your morning and evening rituals based on science so that you have greater control over your day. Rituals like:

- Hydrate before you caffeinate
- Shut of all electronics at least 30 minutes before lights out

Finally, **Community** is the tribe of people you interact with daily. It is where you belong, can be authentic, and where you give and receive accountability so that you co-elevate together. It requires being very clear about how you interact with your community and how your community interacts with you. That means setting boundaries so that others know what is important to YOU. Thus, empowering YOU to take back control.

Creating a life that IGNITES YOU involves a focus on your mindset, lifestyle and community. This journey is for high-performing business leaders who are ready to step into their fullest being as humans and to be truly fulfilled and aligned in all aspects of their lives. Even the smallest steps can shift your life and health in ways you may have never dreamed possible!

Craig Bruce is a former burned-out global executive who struggled with exhaustion, poor sleep, inconsistent food choices and not feeling confident in his own skin. Now, as a Performance & Lifestyle Consultant, he guides other high-performing business leaders and entrepreneurs to get even more from their life without sacrificing their career and key relationships. His IGNITE YOU Programs are transforming the lives of business leaders globally.

Queen of Hearts

Q♥ Teresa Rand

I contribute my business success to my experience as a marathon runner. Having completed eleven marathons, I know first-hand what it takes to go the distance. I believe life, professionally and personally, is a marathon, not a sprint!

My three lessons from training and running, which I use in life and business, are discipline, consistency, and preparation.

Training for a marathon requires **discipline**. You must commit to the training and lifestyle required to complete the course. Discipline is my favorite word! My favorite discipline definition is:

"Activity, exercise, or a regimen that develops or improves a skill: training."
~www.thefreedictionary.com

Everything we do involves discipline; getting up in the morning, going to work, writing that report and turning it in on time, taking an extra class or certification, being a lifelong learner, and helping others along the way. All of these take discipline every day! Discipline is more than habits. It is doing what needs to be done to reach your goals and dreams, no matter what.

Marathon training requires **consistency**. Getting out of bed at 5 AM to run when the weather is freezing is not fun, but if you are going to succeed, you must be consistent even on the hard days. Consistency is a lesson that is easy to understand but not always easy to implement. It is showing up every day, even when you do not want to. Being consistent shows others that you are committed and will do what you say you will do. It is an essential piece of the success puzzle.

Preparation is key to success! It is impossible to run a marathon without preparation. It takes regimented schedules prepared in advance; figuring out your nutrition, your clothes, and your route all require advanced preparation. The same is true for life and business. One must prepare. What are your goals? How will you get there? What do you need? I use the RAND method formula to determine my goals and how I will reach them.

Below is a short version of this method. If you want more information on this, please get in touch with me at tmaxrand@gmail.com.

R: What is your **Reality** right now, and what do you want to change?

A: What **Actions** do you need to take to make this change?

N: What do you **Need** to work toward the change?

D: What is your **Desired** outcome?

No one rolls out of bed one morning and runs 26.2 miles! It takes discipline, consistency, and preparation. No one becomes the CEO in a day. It takes discipline, consistency, and preparation! Executing these three words is the key to success. They each work together to create the life you want!

Discipline + Consistency + Preparation = Success

Teresa Rand is the former CEO of a ten-million-dollar nonprofit. Today she is a successful entrepreneur as the founder and CEO of Teresa Rand Consulting, a firm specializing in using behavioral assessments to enhance team communication and improve productivity. Teresa is also a keynote speaker and passionate supporter of women in the workplace. In 2020, she began *The Boss Lady Podcast*, which airs each Thursday and focuses on empowering, embracing, and educating all women.

Jack of Hearts

J♥ Dr. Patricia Boulogne

Unlocking High-Performance Health: A Journey to Optimal Well-being and Success

Ever feel burned out? My father taught me that you can't nurture someone else if you don't nurture yourself. After over 10 years of a full-on private practice, I decided to retire, sell out, and move from Cape Cod to Boston. However, something happened that changed my course.

While walking around Boston, I observed something so obvious and in my face: the impact of toxins on people's environment, thoughts, and life traumas. A study released in 2010 by the CDC revealed that all of the '212' suspected potentially dangerous chemicals tested were found in the blood and urine of the 2500 individuals tested. This accumulation of toxins was making people sick. Shockingly, it is estimated that by 2030, 50% of the population will be diagnosed with a chronic disease.

This hit close to home. Following those footsteps was exciting... until he died of a heart attack in 1985 at the age of 67. His passing devastated me for several reasons:

- He died too soon.
- He didn't prioritize healthy eating.
- He neglected to take care of himself.
- He was an executive, entrepreneur, and business owner who led by example.

While studying at Chiropractic College, I often wondered if there was something I could have done to extend his life, leveraging the tools and resources at my disposal. This sparked a deep commitment within me to empower people to achieve high-performance health throughout their lifetime.

I embarked on a journey of diving deeper, asking 'WHY' more often, and finding solutions to challenges. I aimed to get unstuck by implementing strategic solutions with the right mindset, prioritizing health, and adopting behaviors that would help individuals reach their full human potential and important life goals, especially in terms of wellness.

This path led me to write 'WHY... Are You Sick, Fat and Tired?' which became an international bestseller. This book of questions serves as a practical guide, workbook, and advocacy tool, showing individuals where to best invest their time, energy, and money when it comes to improving their health. Taking ownership of your destiny diminishes excuses and keeps you moving forward.

It's important to remember that mindset matters. Where your mind goes, your body follows. Your health and mind are crucial for everything you do. The truth is, you can have a great life without sacrificing your well-being, career, or relationships. There are evidence-based lifestyle solutions that allow you to achieve success.

By implementing the following science-proven formula: Positive Mental Attitude + Positive Mindset + Superior Wellness Initiatives = SUCCESS, you can achieve your greatest goals and dreams. Being in control of your thoughts, habits, health, well-being, and happiness allows you to live longer and better, creating the life you've always dreamed of. This is crucial for your immediate and future well-being.

How do you know if you're in sync?

- Are you overworked, overweight, overwhelmed, and depleted?
- Do you find yourself eating on the run, relying on coffee, fast food, or sweets, and feeling tapped out?
- Is your career consuming you, leaving you with no time for fun or special moments?
- Do you struggle to balance your career, family, parents, and relationships?
- Are you in the best state of health, wellness, and well-being?

If you answered 'yes' to any of the above, know someone, or perhaps this resonates with you, know that there are solutions available and you can do better. I invite you to rediscover yourself and ignite a limitless life with less stress, the right mindset, and harmony with your health.

I am Dr. Pat Boulogne, and I am passionate about empowering business leaders to achieve their goals in less time. Join me on this transformative journey.

Dr. Patricia Boulogne, DC, CCSP, AP, CFMP is a Doctor of Functional Medicine and life strategies. She is also the founder and principle of Health Team Network, a company dedicated to skyrocketing your health, lifestyle, and mindsets with strategies and science-based programs empower you to reach your goals in less time.

Ten of Hearts

10♥ Gina Marie Lokken

Play to Your Strengths

"What leaders have in common is that each really knows their strengths, has developed their strengths, and can call on the right strength at the right time."
- Donald Clifton, Founder & Father of Strengths Based Psychology

When you think of the word "strength", what is the first thing that comes to mind?

You may think of bodybuilders like Arnold Schwarzenegger or endurance athletes like Lance Armstrong. Personally, I think of the 1974 boxing match between Muhammad Ali and George Foreman.

Dubbed "*The Rumble in the Jungle*", this heavyweight match-up was meant to be an opportunity for the undisputed champion,

George Foreman, to show his strength. Foreman was more muscular and younger than Ali and was favored to win the match 4-1. However, Ali was faster.

So rather than try to outpunch Foreman, Ali spent the first seven rounds of the match leaning on the ropes and blocking Foreman's punches as the heavy hitter wore himself out. This allowed Ali to come into the eighth round with energy and speed to deliver a barrage of stinging blows that ended in a knockout.[1]

The Rumble in the Jungle is the perfect example of how important it is to focus on and use your unique strengths in order to succeed, even if the odds are stacked against you. By playing to your strengths and using them to your advantage (like Ali) in all facets of life, you improve your results exponentially.

Gallup has conducted numerous studies that challenge the traditional belief that we should focus on improving our weaknesses to succeed. Instead, their research over the last 80 years has consistently shown that investing in and developing our natural talents leads to significantly greater success.

So, do you want better results in your personal and professional life? Here are some time-tested pointers for playing to your strengths and talents:

Identify Your Unique Talents

First, discover your unique talents and how they show up—good, bad, and ugly—in your daily life and interactions. An excellent place to start is with an assessment. The Full 34 CliftonStrengths® Assessment is my personal favorite and the one I believe to be the most reputable, as it's backed by over 80 years of research. Consider the CliftonStrengths® Assessment your secret weapon—a way to identify and develop your unique set of talents immediately!

Play the Hand You've Been Dealt

Don't try to be someone or something you're not; don't "fake it until you make it." You'll only walk away feeling frustrated, defeated, and hollow. Instead, play the hand—the talents—you've been dealt. When you do, your success, happiness, and health will skyrocket. Why? Because when you operate from a place of strength, you will be more energized, fulfilled, and effective—and, most importantly, you'll throw the right punches when it matters.

Nurture Others' Talents

Learn to identify and nurture the talents of others. Sadly, many people downplay the significance of their contributions to the greater good because they do not have encouraging leaders who can help them uncover and develop those talents. Remember:

> *"The more credit you give away, the more will come back to you. The more you help others, the more they want to help you."*
> ~Brian Tracy, Author and Motivational Speaker

Playing to your strengths will make you more happy, successful, and productive!

Citation Information

[1]Article Title: Muhammad Ali wins the Rumble in the Jungle / Author History.com Editors / Website Name: HISTORY / URL https://www.history.com/this-day-in-history/muhammad-ali-wins-the-rumble-in-the-jungle / Access Date December 26, 2022 / Publisher A&E Television Networks / Last Updated: October 26, 2021 / Original Published Date: November 16, 2009

Gina Marie Lokken is an expert at building strengths-based leaders and teams by using neuroscience techniques, leadership and communication training, and cutting-edge coaching methods. She is dedicated to giving business leaders and their teams the tools they need to find and use their unique skills in ways that honor God and their individuality.

Nine of Hearts

9♥ Tracy Brown

Make Inclusion Your Secret Weapon

If you think you are too busy to pay attention to diversity, you are ignoring one of the most valuable resources you have access to. Diversity refers to the variety in humanity. Diversity is simply all the ways we are different from one another both genetically and culturally.

Many people mistakenly think diversity is just about race and gender. Many are convinced if you are talking about diversity, you are talking about discrimination, political power, or competition for limited resources. In reality, valuing diversity is focused on recognizing the people you come into contact with and combining their talent and experience with your own to achieve your commonly shared goals.

Think of the best leaders you have worked with. Unless they have built their success by focusing on fear tactics and power-mongering, most strong leaders have learned to build win-win relationships with a wide variety of people. Great leaders are able to get people to follow them because they have developed a reputation for being respectful of people in different roles and have inspired trust.

In the multicultural, multi-ethnic, and multi-generational world we live in, you can't afford to discount, disregard or disparage people who are different from you. You can never predict when what they know, or who they know, might be the exact information or contact you need.

Don't be fooled by someone's appearance or your perception of their socioeconomic level. Don't assume because someone graduated from an Ivy League school that they know what they are talking about. Be careful about selecting colleagues based on how similar they are to you or how comfortable you are when you are with them. What if the person you are shying away from could introduce you to the buyer of your dreams or the product idea that would transform your business?

To make inclusion your secret weapon, it's not necessary to create different rules of engagement for each person. What's helpful is for you to become curious about different perspectives. What's required is to be open to different approaches or solutions than the ones you would think of.

Starting today, intentionally expand your network. Seek out professional colleagues or leaders in your community who are culturally different from you. Develop relationships with a few people who are at least 20 years older (or younger) than you. Become actively engaged with a community organization in a different part of town. Participate in events where you can learn about different cultural norms.

If you think inclusion is just a game to be played to be politically correct, you are missing the point. You are contributing to more polarity and division in the world. You are slowing down your own success.

Inclusion is not a game; it is a game changer!

Helping leaders demonstrate their commitment to inclusion is a priority for **Tracy Brown**. Her passion is helping individuals build effective cross-cultural relationships that support their personal and professional goals. And her talent is transforming conversations about diversity from a debate about politics and personalities into a dialogue about relationships and results.

Eight of Hearts

8♥ Rosaline Gordon

Planning is often referred to as a detailed proposal, the intention or decision of what one is going to do, to decide on and arrange in advance, and my favorite, a project or definite purpose. Planning is a tool when done with the right people provides valuable insight, support, and a roadmap to a solution. You can use planning to zone in on smaller tasks that will eventually lead you to your ultimate goals, ultimate and meaningful goals that cultivate your purpose. Once the purpose is cultivated, you can change the lives of the people that need you.

Planning Plays an Important Role in Success

Planning commands accountability. Our resources are best used when planning is an intricate part of our decisions. Planning lays the foundation for us to evaluate our practical goals and turn them into wins.

Plan to Profit

Entrepreneurs and small business owners love to attend retreats and conferences. Some of us pay high ticket prices as an investment in ourselves and our businesses. We leave inspired, renewed, emotionally, and practically prepared. The next time you plan to attend an event, I would like you to consider how you will get a return on your investment. It is not enough to walk away with the expense. If you are planning an event, plan to profit. You will thank me later when you are no longer worrying about your cash flow.

There is Nothing Wrong with Having a Plan B!

I am the Queen of Plan B! I've heard renowned speakers say all the time, "There is no need for Plan B" or "Plan B sucks". I believe that it is unrealistic. Having a Plan B does not mean you do not have faith in your Plan A, but it does not mean that if you have a Plan B that your Plan A will not work, and it does not cause a distraction. Plan B simply offers you an opportunity to begin again.

Planning is Spiritual

I heard a story of a man who was ill and could not walk. He wanted to go into town to visit a "doctor" who was not going to be in town very long. He told his friends of his desire to go, so the man and his friends (support) planned to go. When they got there for a remedy, they could not fathom the number of people that were there for the same thing (a solution). He was going to turn around, but his friends came up with another plan. They decided to climb up to the roof and lower him down so that he could be seen. As a result of their determination, he received his healing, and they were blessed because they did not have to carry him back home. In life, you are going to have crowds and ceilings. things that come up in life deviating you from your plans. It is essential no matter how skilled and resourceful; you must make God the center of your plans so that He can guide you to be in proximity to people and professionals who want to help you succeed so that you can walk in your purpose and show up powerfully for the people that need you.

Lastly, if you fail to plan, you plan to fail. A Plan is only a concept, an idea, or a dream until you EXECUTE.

ROSALINE GORDON – BUSINESS STRATEGIST | ENTREPRENEUR | CHIEF FINANCIAL OFFICER

With over 30 years of experience in optimizing client accounting services, handling tax preparation, resolution, planning, and managing outsourced CFO services, Rosaline Gordon is a prominent financial expert in Iselin, New Jersey.

Since 2015, Rosaline has been the Chief Executive Officer and Founder of The Gordon Financial Services, Inc., an Iselin, New Jersey-based boutique business management firm, tactically overseeing services offered to small business ventures and high-net-worth individuals.

Seven of Hearts

7♥ Lea Hope Bonzer

Success Hacks

I was born and raised in Zagreb, the capital of Croatia. When I was 10 years old, the war in Yugoslavia began. Somehow it felt like a game, the excitement of something new, but why are my parents so scared? It was a confusing time as I was unable to comprehend reality.

Things started changing, but a lot about war went in vain. When sirens blared, it was time for the hideout, but mainly we went on with life as it became the new norm. The war ended, but that was not the end of difficulties. On many levels, it was a beginning. Despair, political greed, injustice, government corruption, and lack of opportunities took over. I have always been a big dreamer. My dad used to joke about, "little Lea dreaming about the big world" but I was dying inside with each day passing. I had to escape. I made a journey with one suitcase and zero expectations. It was not an easy journey, there were many nights of tears, and many moments of shocking mistakes through recognizing the cultural differences, which I was not aware of.

I started out to become an artist, but photographing my children has pivoted my goal to becoming a portrait photographer instead. I enjoy capturing moments and feeling as they happen, so becoming a portrait photographer is amazing but being an artist was still alive in me.

As my business was taking off, the family received orders for a one-year move, which turned into two.

It was great to have this opportunity to create more art within new places. I got to travel where I never thought I would, but I wasn't ready to give up on my portrait photography business or on my dream to be an artist.

After returning, I was eager to start my business again. In March 2020, COVID took root throughout the world and put my business on a break, again. I used that time to finally gather all my art and create a website. I set myself on the mission to enchant surroundings either residential, commercial, or hospitality, and implement the design with motivation and inspiration. Pushing myself out of my comfort zone, I started networking. Networking has changed my life. I partnered up on customized ceiling tiles to ease unpleasant doctor's visits. This led to mural designs. With my art, I also created a dangling earring line. The book I wrote for my children as a Christmas gift, about a baby bunny we rescued, found an actual publisher. I have learned, not just through networking, but through all my life experiences so far, to never allow the emotions of the day to determine the future of my life.

Lea Hope Bonzer is an award-winning artist and founder of Hope Decor. Lea's mission is to recreate and energize the ambiance of interiors. Lea is also a portrait and event photographer, an author of a children's bedtime storybook, and recently started dangling earring lines with her art printed on them.

Six of Hearts

6♥ Dr. Lamarr Renee Spencer

Life Hacks for Business and Life

In today's fast-paced world, finding effective strategies to navigate the challenges of both business and personal life is crucial. Here are some life hacks or recommendations that can prove useful in various aspects:

1. **Don't Rush:** One of the most common life pitfalls is making hasty decisions. Unless there is an immediate emergency, take the time for careful reflection and consideration. By avoiding rushed choices, you can make more informed decisions that lead to better outcomes.

2. **Think Twice:** It's essential to exercise caution when communicating online. Before sending that email or posting a comment, think twice. Avoid posting messages when feeling anxious, stressed, or upset, as it can lead to regrettable consequences. Remember, once something is posted online, it's difficult to retract it completely. Some may even say, "The internet is forever."

3. **Socialize:** Engaging with like-minded individuals or those who share similar interests can have a profound impact on your well-being. By spending time socializing, you can decompress your mind, gain new perspectives, and find motivation. Building a network of supportive family and friends can be instrumental in both business and personal growth.

4. **Balance:** Striking a balance between work and personal life is vital for overall well-being. Organize your schedules, duties, and responsibilities in a way that allows for harmonious coexistence. A balanced approach reduces stress and anxiety, enhances productivity, and provides a sense of accomplishment in various areas of life.

5. **Plan:** While not everyone is naturally inclined towards planning, it is an invaluable tool for tackling major projects. Break down complex tasks into smaller, manageable portions and set milestones along the way. This approach makes even the most daunting undertakings appear less overwhelming, increasing your chances of success.

By adopting these life hacks, you can improve your decision-making process, maintain a positive online presence, foster meaningful connections, achieve work-life balance, and effectively manage your projects. Remember, implementing these strategies takes practice and dedication, but the long-term benefits are well worth the effort.

In a world full of distractions and constant demands, having a set of life hacks can significantly enhance your personal and professional life. Take the time to reflect on your decision-making, be mindful of your online communications, prioritize social connections, seek balance in all areas, and embrace the power of planning. By incorporating these recommendations into your routine, you can unlock greater success, happiness, and fulfillment in both business and life.

Dr. Lamarr Renee Spencer is a Life Alignment Strategist with 25+ years of professional business experience. She specializes in helping burned-out business owners streamline operations, restore balance, and enjoy important moments. As a public speaker, she shares her insights and empowers others to take charge of their lives.

Five of Hearts

5♥ Sally Wurr

"You must take personal responsibility.
You cannot change the circumstances, the seasons,
or the wind, but you can change yourself."
-Jim Rohn

Success has a different meaning for each person. Some people define success as having a certain amount of money in their bank account. Other people define success based on the number of people they can call friends.

For me, success means a little bit of both. I like to feel comfortable with a certain amount of money in my bank account and I also like to surround myself with people that have similar interests as mine and are heading in a direction I want to go.

I built my second company utilizing the following principles. It helped me keep my focus. Whenever I found myself floundering and wondering what I needed to do next, I would pause and go back to the original principles that helped me get where

I was. Sometimes when we find the "magic" of success, we forget and lose our way. We forget what got us where we are.

My "go to" list has five principles that I remind myself of when I am beginning a new journey or lose my way on the current one. I will share them with you, and it is my hope it will help you.

Principle # 1:

Clarify your vision of what you want. You need to know where you are now and where you want to go. Create a detailed list of what your vision looks like.

Principle # 2:

Set goals for your journey. In order to have the best outcome, you need to break down these goals into bite-size pieces to be tackled separately.

The best way is to figure out a tracking system. This way you know where to begin, the steps you need to take in the middle and what a successful outcome looks like. If you fail to complete the entire process, you will not have the success you had hoped for.

You need a starting point. Decide on a plan, define the steps and place them in the correct order, then complete the goal.

If there is anything new you want in your life, you must make room for it, physically and psychologically.

According to many successful business people, you need to follow the four "D"s.

Do it, Delegate it, Delay it, or Dump it.

Principle # 3:

Decide the importance of a project. When distractions arrive, and they always do, ask yourself if it gets you closer to your goal or further away? Always do the important steps first and work on decreasing distractions.

Principle # 4:

When you are quoting someone or posting photos from special events, do your best to share your appreciation with those who have helped you get where you are. Make sure you publicly thank them and make sure you spell their name correctly. Everyone likes to see their photo and hear their name, so use them often.

Principle # 5:

Do not assume people are doing things to you on purpose. Too many people get offended quickly if something does not go their way or they feel slighted. I have also seen people get upset as they feel they were snubbed at an event. Most likely, you were not "snubbed"; that other person probably had something else on their mind and either didn't see you or hear you. Most things in life are NOT about you.

The strongest people have their own doubts and fears. Give everyone some grace. They do what they can and may forget things.

"See what you want, get what you see."
-Author unknown

Sally Wurr has spent her life challenging herself and others to step outside their comfort zones. Her strength lies in sharing and teaching others how to design a life they want.

Sally is an International Speaker, Multi-book Author and Coach. Her latest books are a trilogy. The Power of Awakening, The Power of Purpose and The Power of Legacy will help you figure out who you were meant to be and the steps to get there.

You can reach Sally by following her on Facebook or by going to her website www.SallyWurr.com. You will be able to follow where Sally will be speaking next and when her books are available.

Four of Hearts

4♥ Margie Dunki-Jacobs

7 Life Hacks to Crush it With Confidence and Win in Life!

1. **Create your standards** of how you choose to live your life and let them be your solid foundation in all that you do.

2. **DWYSYGTD**. Do What You Say You're Going to Do. When you can count on your word, others count on you and this creates enormous confidence not only in yourself but in others' trust in your confidence.

3. **Be determined**. You must be able to make a decision, commit to it, and take focused massive action on your decision. You will succeed when you are fully committed to your decision. Know what you want to achieve and why you want to achieve it. Then write it down! When you are discouraged, reconnect to your why and re-energize your efforts. Be unstoppable.

4. **Let go of what other people think of you!** Protect your dreams with a positive attitude bubble around you and the

people who support you. Be unpoppable. All of these come in first place, but this boosts your confidence 10X! They don't have your dreams, your heart, your desire, your life! You can be supported by people, liked and disliked, but it's all neutral. It's just feedback that you can choose to use to elevate your life! Be detached from the likes and the negative comments! Just keep focused.

5. **Build positive relationships**! Find something good in people! Some people make it very challenging to find something good in them, but when you are able to find something good in others, you rise above the judgment! It doesn't mean everyone is allowed in your life or business. Let go of the negative ones! Build rich relationships with the positive ones.

6. **You must STOP the negative talk and replace it with positive "how can I?" talk!** Take an 8.5 x 11 sheet of paper. Draw a line horizontally across the center. Write down all the negative ways you talk to yourself below the line and choose to live above the line. Write down above the line the solution-based positive talk, life is about what's possible! Destroy the negative talk (i.e., "we are never going to find a parking space in this crowd." "It's no use. I'll never be able to be good at...."). You must figure out what you can do and how you can do it. Start from there.

7. **Get an experienced coach and get involved in a community, not of like-minded people, but of growth-minded people**. Plug in for one year with everything you've got. You will crush it with confidence! You have the ability to explode your relationships to a 10 out of a 10, live truly joyfully, and add life-changing income to your bank account!

Keynote Inspirational Speaker, Bestselling Author, Confidence Breakthrough Coach and Wealth Strategist, **Margie Dunki-Jacobs** helps clients break through all limiting beliefs to experience powerful liberating beliefs with one unique exercise that gives them the confidence they must have in order to achieve the success and income they desire.

Three of Hearts

3♥ John Diggs

Sometimes necessity truly is the mother of invention. The best success hack I ever created came out of the lowest point of my life when I made the decision to apply Mind Mapping to my rock-bottom life circumstances. After losing my business, family, and home, I made the life-changing decision to try using Mind Mapping on a personal level. This hack allowed me to rebuild every aspect of my life. In fact, I was able to go from zero to sixty in four months. Let me explain.

After losing everything, I was determined to apply advice from the greatest thinkers of our time to my personal life. I had read many of their books and taken many of their courses over the course of several years. What I learned helped me build my successful mortgage software company after retiring from a pro football career. But none of that wisdom protected me from the mortgage meltdown of 2008. I knew the concepts these thought leaders taught had value, but I also knew that I needed a more effective way to keep track of key points and recall the details of their multiple suggestions and ideas. Mind Mapping all that information allowed me to do just that.

I had heard about Mind Maps before, but, like many of us, never used them. Even though Mind Maps had been around for centuries and were successfully used in top business and university settings, I had never known how powerful they could be.

What I discovered when I made the decision to use them to record all the key concepts from all my books and educational materials was that mind maps allowed me to use non-linear thinking and enabled me to recognize connections between different pieces of information. I could quickly see key points much better than with traditional notetaking I had used in the past. I no longer had to try to memorize key bits of information because when I glanced at the Mind Maps I created, my brain quickly recalled all the information. It was a staggering discovery for me.

Mind Maps also gave me a broader understanding and more holistic view of concepts and topics. I found that I could easily update and modify my Mind Maps, which made them an ideal tool for brainstorming and capturing thoughts and ideas as they evolved over time. Creating mind maps of personal goals, aspirations, and ambitions also helped me to clarify and prioritize my objectives. By visually mind mapping out my path to success, for my business, I have been able to track progress, identify potential obstacles, and make necessary adjustments along the way.

On a personal level, Mind Mapping has allowed me to get very clear about who I AM, to pinpoint exactly what it takes for me to truly Love Life and to transform those ideals into my personal reality.

LA-born former pro football player turned mortgage software developer, author, speaker, and leader of an online community, **John Diggs** has experienced many highs of success. It was the low of failure, however, that fostered the life-changing idea that led him to become one of the world's top authorities in Mind Mapping.

Two of Hearts

2♥ Cat Oshman

Living an Inspired Life: How confidence, inspiration, and faith lead to a life with purpose, fulfillment, and success

Have you ever felt stuck in a rut with your career, business… or life in general? What were the pivotal moments that helped transform your life?

Living an inspired life is something that people strive for, but not all are able to achieve. It can be difficult to find purpose and fulfillment in your daily routine, especially when you feel like you are just going through the motions. However, with a spark of confidence and courage, it's possible to transform your life into one that is truly inspiring and filled with joy.

First and foremost, confidence is key when it comes to living an inspired life. Having self-belief and a positive mindset can help you overcome obstacles that come your way. When you're confident in your abilities, you're more likely to take risks and pursue goals that are more challenging. This can lead to a more fulfilling life, inspiring you to take action to create the life you want rather than waiting for things to happen.

Taking risks and embracing change can often be scary, but it is necessary to grow and achieve success. Making bolder moves leads to new opportunities and experiences.

How do you cultivate these qualities in your own life?

1. In the beginning, start small and set achievable goals for yourself. Celebrate your successes along the way. This will build up your confidence and help develop a growth mindset. Embrace the timing of your life. If you only focus on the end goal, you create negative energy from one milestone to the next, never truly appreciating the journey.

2. Surround yourself with positive influences and people who inspire you. I find value in joining network communities that are on similar growth journeys. They are people you can collaborate with and hold each other accountable. One of the actions I have taken that has been pivotal in my success is finding key mentors that help expand my leadership techniques, communication, and additional transferrable skills that open the aperture for growth. Interactive mentors open the door to their network and optimize your vision for the future.

3. Do something different and expand your perspective through the experience. Personally, I love to travel, experience different cultures, talk to people, find out

where they're from and how they live. Creative and amazing ideas have come from leaving town. To maximize this experience, limit the time on your electronics. This increases your capacity to receive what the world is opening for you. Have a great time! One of the things I did outside of my comfort zone was being an extra in a film. I was nervous and excited at the same time. Ask yourself, what am I learning? What have I learned? What area am I expanding my life?

Embracing your uniqueness and defining success on your own terms go hand in hand when living an inspired life. By staying true to yourself and pursuing goals that resonate with your values, you can achieve a sense of purpose and fulfillment that will motivate you to keep pushing forward. Radical acceptance that the road to success is not a straight line.

Cat Oshman is a success-proven executive, recognized swimwear designer, confidence catalyst, and founder of AMEN Show (Amplified Moms Empowerment Network). Cat is known for her exceptional leadership skills and unwavering commitment to empowering women. As the VP of Design, she has played a pivotal role in shaping the visual identity of numerous brands. Cat has traveled the globe for inspiration and can be seen gracing red carpets with celebrities and influencers.

SPADES

The spade represents a leaf of the "cosmic" tree, and thus, life. Along with its companion suit, clubs, spades represent fall and winter and the power of darkness. In the Tarot, they symbolize intellect, action, air, and death.

~ www.fleurdelis.com/symbols

Ace of Spades

A♠ Michele Marshall

The ace of spades is the most iconic playing card within a traditional deck. Sometimes printed with a blank face, skull, or skeleton, the card became associated with death and superstition. However, the ace of spades also has a more positive connotation - representing good luck, power, and fortune.

Your Ace of Spades is Customer Service.

The death or wealth of your business rests upon the level of customer service provided.

Within any business, customer service is a vital building block for customer retention, client referrals, and a company's reputation. An essential step for success is to give your customers an exceptional caring experience. Specifically, providing a **P**atient, **U**nderstanding, **R**espectful **E**xperience [P.U.R.E].

Whether you're a representative, a manager, or an entrepreneur, take pride in the business of serving customers. By implementing a Patient, Understanding, Respectful Experience, you can foster genuine person-to-person connections in which you care for your customer and the company's bottom line. Remember, it is only through customer service that a company can have its finger on the pulse of its customers' overall wants and needs. Excellent customer service should be the *norm* - it shouldn't be an exception. Every position within a company that involves customer interaction must be treated as a customer service position because you interact with people daily and impact their life experiences. Treating someone like they matter is always worth the effort, and the returns are exponential.

Excellence in customer service is about showing the customer you care about them and their experience with your product/services. By turning reactive inquiries into proactive results while advocating for your customer's satisfaction, customer service becomes a powerful lifeline. People shouldn't expect customer service representatives to be rude. Customers should always be able to assume they will receive exceptional service from you and your company. As an industry, we must course-correct the tainted perception of customer service. We should welcome our customers and assure them that when they talk, we will listen. Let's make kindness the standard.

It's important to note that customers reaching out to your business is good, even with the bad apples. Customer interaction allows you to retool your product and services in order to raise customer satisfaction. Such interactions tell you what your company is and isn't doing right. Feedback from your customers should be accepted and encouraged.

I challenge you to set the standard in your field for customer service. It is up to you to be the trailblazer for this revolution of creating a Patient, Understanding, and Respectful Experience for your customers.

It is our privilege to show these people that there is someone in the world who cares about them. Customer service can become a space where people experience a basic level of empathy and respect that we should all get. We are the people who help to make the world a little more caring and a little kinder.

A company's profits hinge on its customer service experience. Hence, the Ace of Spades for Success is Customer Service.

Michele Marshall, CPC; professional coach, trainer, and speaker; customer care expert; and author of Happy to Help: The Lost Art of Customer Service. Her mission is to equip professionals with the skillset to strengthen their communication and customer service skills.

King of Spades

K♠ Seth Miller

3 Things You Need to Maintain Success

We all have different definitions of what success is. In this chapter, I would like to point to three things that have been prevalent for many people and attributed to their success. These three things are having the right people around you, acceptance of reality, and a certain mindset.

Have the Right People Around You

At the age of 42, I've come to the realization that I won't get along with everybody. I should be picky with my company – and I'm cool with that! My circle is very important to me. A key to success is having a solid team and family in your corner. No matter what you think, you can't do it all by yourself.

Along with grit and determination, carefully selecting those by our side can have an immense impact on how successful that ride ends up being. Though it may be uncomfortable at times, being honest and making sure our relationships are built on trust is essential. Life is ever-changing, so it pays off to stay mindful of our various relationships – whether professional or personal. Pay attention to who you're spending your time with and evaluate how different situations are impacting your well-being and progress.

Accept Reality

Life is going to happen to us and these experiences will help us grow. How we accept our current situation will give us a direction to the next destination. Even if we feel desperate at times, it is important to look for the lessons and takeaways from each experience. We can then use them as stepping stones towards a better tomorrow. Furthermore, understanding that there are positive aspects to every situation will help us cope and move forward with optimism.

Create a Growth Mindset

Pushing yourself to try new things, learning more and challenging yourself isn't easy. However, with the right mindset, a growth mindset, you are able to accept feedback for what it is—a learning opportunity that helps you grow in your desired direction. Don't give up when the going gets tough. Instead, use the difficulty as an opportunity to form new strategies and think outside of the box.

Above all else, maintaining success depends upon having an attitude of resilience; no matter what obstacles arise, there is always a way to overcome them. With the right people, perspective, and mental fortitude, success can be achieved and sustained.

Seth "The Speaker" Miller is a professional speaker and author of The Black Collar Mindset where he provides the perfect tools for you to take your dreams or goals to the next level. Seth is a retired US Air Force Master Sergeant of 21 years, and the current Commander of his local VFW post 4183. He's also a podcast producer and host of The Lion's Den with Seth, and Healed with Seth the Speaker that are available on all major podcast platforms, with an international audience. When he's not spending time with family, Seth enjoys opportunities to speak at schools, conferences, and veteran-focused events.

Queen of Spades

Q♠ Phyllis Caddell

Hacks to Succeed as an Entrepreneur and Enhance Your Business

Are you an entrepreneur who aspires to achieve success? Do you ever feel you're not getting the expected results despite putting in the effort? It could be difficult to figure out where to begin. However, success in entrepreneurship requires an unrelenting desire for success and improvement.

Integrating hacks into your routine is a great way to begin your path to success as an entrepreneur. Using hacks can enable entrepreneurs to boost efficiency, distinguish themselves from competitors, and show creativity and innovation.

Being a successful entrepreneur and growing my business as a publicist involves implementing several hacks. Here are six hacks you can try:

1. Build a powerful brand: As a publicist, I know how important branding is. Apply this same expertise to your own business by creating a strong brand identity that differentiates you from your competitors and attracts clients.

Creating a strong brand identity is important because it helps build brand recognition and recall, making it easier for customers to identify and remember your brand. A strong brand identity can also help build trust and credibility with customers.

2. Blogging: By creating and publishing blog content on topics related to your business, you can establish yourself as an expert in your industry. This can help build trust with potential customers and clients and make it more likely that they will choose to do business with you.

3. Connect with influencers and thought leaders: This provides an opportunity to expand your professional network and connect with individuals who can help you grow your business.

However, it is essential to approach the relationship organically. Providing value, sharing insights, and engaging with their content are ways to build relationships. Cultivating meaningful relationships will benefit your business.

4. Offer value-added services: Offering value-added services to your clients can be an effective way to differentiate yourself from your competitors, provide additional value to your clients, and increase your revenue streams. It is also an effective way to create opportunities to upsell and cross-sell to your existing clients.

5. Embrace automation: Use tools such as scheduling software, email marketing platforms, and social media management tools to streamline your operations and save time. This can help you focus on growing your business and providing value to your clients. It's also important to communicate the benefits of these services to your clients and price them appropriately.

6. Incorporate Artificial Intelligence (AI): Businesses use AI for tasks like customer service and media monitoring. AI-driven tools are enabling entrepreneurs to shift their focus away from mundane tasks and to more creative endeavors like crafting interesting messages and brainstorming innovative strategies.

AI is also used to improve content and reach new customers. Companies can gain market insights by using AI algorithms to process real-time data, leading to more effective, tailored campaigns.

By implementing these hacks, you can position yourself as a successful entrepreneur and build a thriving business.

With a diverse set of skills, **Phyllis Caddell** is an author, ghostwriter, publicist, and communications strategist.

As the founder of PCPR Communications, she has been guiding clients in developing, crafting, and improving their brand narratives for over 25 years.

Her success is attributed to her proficiency in public relations, content development, digital marketing, storytelling, and organizational communications.

She is also a subject matter expert (SME), and adjunct professor for Azusa Pacific University, and holds an M.A. in Organizational Communications, an M.S. in Internet Marketing, and a B.A. in Public Relations.

Jack of Spades

J♠ Ken Lewis

After 20 years of military service, I found myself lost and bewildered. I was searching for a new direction in life and civilian employment. I needed clarity, purpose, and identity. I was losing money and feeling like the walls were crumbling around me. I required a significant change immediately. I knew I needed to claw my way out from rock bottom and become something more meaningful, or I would perish in a dark abyss.

This was the turning point in my post-military life. My identity transformed as I learned about my new purpose. Rather than being an Air Force Master Sergeant bomb technician, I concentrated on being a spouse and a father. The military was no longer my only lifeline, and I had stopped undervaluing what I had learned in the service and instead started utilizing it to my advantage.

I learned how to reclaim control of my life, rediscover meaning, and imagine what success would look like for me in 30 years—no more excuses and no one to blame but myself. I began by creating a personal mission and vision statement and outlining the values and principles that would support the life my family and I wanted and deserved.

After a few self-awareness exercises, I hired a coach, reviewed my skills, strengths, and weaknesses, and rediscovered my interests and passions. I had the basic outline for a new success roadmap. Most significantly, I committed myself to the life and career I desired. I wrote big goals every day. After overcoming my scarcity mindset, I stopped dreaming, thinking, and acting small.

I sought knowledge through reading, online courses, college, and my favorite, interviewing people who have gone where I want to go. I became more intentional with networking, which led to opportunities aligned with my new vision.

It is funny to think that in the military, my job was to discover and render safe unexploded dangers like roadside bombs. Yet as a civilian, I was terrified of an enemy I had created within myself—an imposter syndrome.

If you are facing similar predicaments, my advice is to adopt a growth mindset and be eager to learn. Do not underestimate the effort needed to achieve any goal. Learn to know when you need help and then get it. Never doubt your worth or potential. Roll up your sleeves, take calculated risks, and get uncomfortable. Do not let up once you have gained even the tiniest momentum toward your ideal future; instead, remain vigorous and relentless. Get out there and build a network to create an added support system of like-minded individuals.

You have the skills, discipline, and determination to thrive in any field. Do not let anything hold you back from achieving your goals. Be confident and stay committed to long-term success and financial wealth.

Ken Lewis is a highly experienced coach, consultant, and facilitator with over two decades of experience in leadership development, professional skills training, and personal growth coaching. He is a U.S. Air Force veteran and a former Explosive Ordnance Disposal team leader. He holds various certifications, including PMP, CMQ/OE, and Prosci Change Practitioner. Ken's unique background makes him well-suited to help with a range of issues, including business improvement, organizational and people development, and team dynamics.

Ten of Spades

10♠ David A. Aviles

Imagine a journey where you can unlock the secrets to a fulfilling life and a successful career. Along the way, you encounter valuable lessons and insights that can guide you towards your goals and empower you to realize your true potential. Here are some of those transformative discoveries that attributed to my success.

As you embark on your path, embrace a growth mindset. Embrace the belief that you have the power to develop your skills and capabilities continuously. Approach challenges as opportunities for growth and learning. By maintaining an open and positive mindset, you'll be prepared to seize the possibilities that come your way.

In your pursuit of success, recognize the importance of collaboration and teamwork. Foster an environment that encourages open communication, values diverse perspectives, and builds strong relationships based on trust and respect. When you harness the collective power of a team, you'll find that together, you can accomplish far more than you could alone.

Never stop investing in your own development. Seek out opportunities for continuous learning, whether through professional development programs, workshops, or certifications. Stay up to date with industry trends and constantly sharpen your skills. This dedication to growth will keep you ahead in your career and open doors to new opportunities.

Networking and building relationships are essential components of success. Connect with like-minded professionals, attend industry events, and join relevant associations. Cultivate a strong professional network that can offer support, guidance, and potential collaborations. Don't be afraid to both seek mentorship from experienced individuals and mentor others who can benefit from your knowledge and expertise.

Crafting a strong personal brand is crucial in a competitive job market. Develop a polished resume, create a professional online presence, and cultivate a compelling elevator pitch that effectively communicates your unique value proposition. By showcasing your skills, accomplishments, and expertise, you'll stand out from the crowd and attract opportunities aligned with your aspirations.

While pursuing your goals, remember to maintain a healthy work-life balance. Set boundaries and prioritize self-care. Allocate time for activities that bring you joy and fulfillment outside of work. Striking this balance will prevent burnout and sustain your long-term success and well-being.

In your journey towards success, remember to give back and make a positive impact. Volunteer, mentor, or participate in social impact initiatives. Sharing your knowledge and experiences not only benefits others but also enhances your own personal and professional growth. By lifting others up, you create a ripple effect of positive change.

As you embrace these life and career hacks, know that you have the power to transform your own life. Combine the wisdom gained from these lessons with your unique experiences and passions. Write your own narrative of success, making a positive impact on your communities and achieving the fulfillment you deserve.

David A. Aviles is an award-winning executive leader with a transformative track record in the public and private sectors. Currently Manager of Development at Manhattan Neighborhood Network (MNN), he's recognized for empowering communities, driving change, and fostering youth success. He's also an author and founder of CareerReadyResume.com, a respected career consulting firm.

Nine of Spades

9♠ Marcy Myles-Clark

Embracing Total Wellness for Maximum Success

As a Financial wellness strategist (with over 20 years of experience) who's overcome many of life's unexpected curveballs, I feel compelled to share tidbits of my personal experiences and professional expertise. I'm obliged to share this information as a means of giving back and helping others to eliminate the many pitfalls that often hold us back. I believe that God delivers us through situations so that we can be a blessing to others. I challenge you to read this chapter with an open mind and to embrace and implement what is necessary for your total wellness in order to achieve maximum entrepreneurial and personal success.

During these uncertain post-pandemic times filled with war stories, inflation, crime, immigration, political mayhem and more, I found myself—like so many others—frustrated, searching for answers, ready to reclaim the life we once knew, and wanting to get back to normal. I discovered that many of the comforts that we enjoyed previously have been indefinitely suspended, and many will become memories of the past that we won't ever reclaim. Instead of being bitter about what I lost, I chose to embrace the new norm and some of the positives that have been born over the last three-and-a-half years—which reminds me of the Christian serenity prayer. I fully embrace this prayer spiritually; however, from a practical perspective I think the biggest takeaway as it relates to modern times lies within the first sentence:

"God, grant me the serenity
to accept the things I cannot change,
the courage to change the things I can,
and the wisdom to know the difference."
-Reinhold Niebuhr

As we move forward to reclaim our victory, these words help us to recognize what we can and cannot change, to accept the unchangeable (although we may not fully understand or agree with it), and to focus on the things that are within our power to change. By redirecting our thoughts and our energy to focus on the things we CAN change, we free up our minds (firstly) to focus on more productive tasks. Once we've set our minds FREE, we can accomplish the impossible, as we've seen throughout history. A free or unencumbered mind is a fruitful mind which harvests many positive outcomes.

Typically, once our minds are in check, our bodies and our spirits will follow, giving us a sense of "total wellness". This peaceful synchronization of mind, body, and spirit is what I refer to as the "WholeSum (total) approach" which consists of strategies that we can utilize to obtain total wellness. Some include embracing the power of preparation and implementing resources for peace of mind etc.; these give us a sense of confidence and lead us closer to obtaining total wellness and maximum success.

I've planted some seeds in this chapter to help you think about your total wellness, and I've presented some WholeSum approach tactics to maximize your personal and professional successes. Please keep in touch to further discuss these and more strategies.

Marcy Myles-Clark, MBA is a best-selling author and Financial Wellness Strategist who's overcome many of life's unexpected curveballs. Marcy empowers others by mentoring, coaching, and speaking on "total wellness" strategies, including "The Power of Preparation" and "Resources for Peace of Mind." Marcy is also the founder of CoverYourAssetsIns.com

Eight of Spades

8♠ Stephen Boyd

At the last wedding I attended, I recall listening to the bride and groom recite their vows. "I, ___, take thee, ___, to be my wedded husband/wife/spouse, to have and to hold from this day forward, for better, for worse, for richer, for poorer, in sickness and in health, to love and to cherish, till death do us part." In addition to the traditional vows, each recited custom vows to each other to personalize and solidify their commitment to each other.

Commitment? A word that causes some to smile and others to cringe! Yet, without commitment glue wouldn't hold together a broken vase. Without commitment, roads and bridges would crumble. Without commitment, a house would not stand. Without commitment, a business cannot be successful. To be committed to something means to make an agreement, pledge, or do something in the future. Individuals who want to be successful in life and business should consider making three commitments if they want to be successful in life and business. They are a commitment to prayer and meditation, a commitment to focus, and a commitment to strategic planning.

As an entrepreneur, committing to prayer and meditation helps to keep you grounded during the highs and lows of your business life cycle. Whether it's a disgruntled customer, a potential client that backs out of a deal, or the joy of landing the deal of a lifetime, committing to prayer and meditation provides you with a foundation to remain committed to your core values. Which leads me to my next commitment, a commitment to focus.

John Maxwell says, "He who aims at nothing will hit it every time." Invariably as an entrepreneur, you'll want to experiment with different thoughts, ideas, products, or services that you feel provide value to others. When your business is in its infancy, it is normal to engage in this sort of experimentation. However, as your business grows in order to broaden your influence you must narrow your focus. You must ask yourself, "Where does my business provide the greatest value?" "To whom does my business provide the greatest value?" As you answer those questions and evaluate your business's analytics, narrow your attention to that value and 'turn up the heat' on your transformation!

Finally, there is a commitment to strategic planning. While this is a cadence no one wants to play, it's certainly a rhythm that guides you toward success! There is an ancient proverb that says, 'If you fail to plan, you plan to fail.' I certainly had my fair share of failures in life and in business. But as I've increased my commitment to strategic planning (including working with a planning coach) I've seen exponential growth in my life and business!

As CEO of SB Entertainment, LLC, **Stephen Boyd** is a motivational speaker, K-12 trainer, and consultant who's been impacting others in the sectors of education, faith, and business for nearly 30 years. His life mission is to increase the leadership value of others by educating their minds, exciting their hearts, and empowering their hands!

Seven of Spades

7♠ Nadia Hayes Simmons

I wrote my first book called ***Smiles*** because I wanted to be an advocate, activist, and ambassador for the youth and those affected by mental illnesses, sexual assault, gun violence, cyberbullying, suicides, and Roe vs Wade. I became a writer as well because it provided an opportunity for me to describe the world in ways we don't usually see it. I wanted to write for a sense of accomplishment by having a book published. Writing for me was therapeutic because it allowed more meaningful transparency and thoughtfulness within myself to bring awareness and change through my own personal traumas and experiences. As I am growing up in a working-class neighborhood in Georgia, I developed a thick skin and a disciplined approach to discerning people's pain and perspectives. It's easy to lose hope in our culture, to think everything is meaningless, to give up on the world and just chase after my own pleasure. This motivated me to find a path to fight against these ills that are bleeding our communities domestically and globally.

This has helped me tremendously to be better at learning my strengths, weaknesses, patience, empathy, serving, healing, growing, and loving as a human being. It is inspiring and an amazing way to give life through words and to enter the deepest part of becoming better. This is what I have learned to help shape and move me through the lens of my perspectives.

I personally feel that my mission is to affect a positive outlook and to foster insight. Also, speak to the hearts and be the voice of individuals who are quiet with their private thoughts. To help someone feel less alone. This book is to evoke compassion even among strangers and to create opportunities to understand others better and cultivate empathy towards them. What they can learn or walk away with is to spread love, hope, peace, unity, and compassion for each other. This can affect the youth and others but build stronger youth future leaders, strengthen our communities by sharing my experiences and traumas with other youths, and instill the importance of moral values and making responsible choices. This is about empowering and evolving every person. Inspiring and nurturing the human spirit and changing the world. I want my readers to know that we all have a s story in us. I am interested in helping others. If I can help just one person reach their goals as a better human being or a writer, I have achieved what I set out to do.

Your LEGACY is not what you leave with people, your LEGACY is what you leave inside people.

Nadia Hayes Simmons is a teenage author and screenwriter with a passion for sharing stories that will inspire others, especially youth, during times of struggle with the challenges of life. She has written and published a book, called Smiles, in which she shares her own life experiences and how she has worked hard to become a stronger, more resilient young person, and an advocate for positive change in a difficult world.

Six of Spades

6♠ Teresa Mack

The road to success is paved with solid cornerstones, such as clear goals, resilient determination, routines, systems, and accountability.

An entrepreneur's success is short-lived without establishing the cornerstones, despite having talent, vision, creativity, and luck. After a career in public accounting, I went on to be a successful attorney, mother, real estate broker, manager, and by most accounts a successful woman, but I didn't become a successful entrepreneur until I did these things.

THINK BIGGER and set goals that are audacious and unreal. You limit your potential with shallow goals and weak thinking. Level up and think big. If you're cruising through an endeavor, you're not achieving your full potential.

NEVER GIVE UP. I can promise you your biggest successes are on the other side of failure. When you feel resistance, know that you are closer to success.

CREATE STRUCTURE AND ROUTINE and stick to them – modify when appropriate, but do not let up. Your competition will overtake you.

Structure – A set of steps that lead reliably to a result that brings you closer to your goal. Whether it's a listing checklist to manage hundreds of listings simultaneously at a high level or a daily walk and meditations that ensure you are on top of your game every day - structure is a must.

Routine – The act of consistently repeating a task, action, or set thereof.

"You can't con **consistency**." The owner of our brokerage has a few catchphrases that keep me on track – this is one of them. When an agent comes to me in distress because they are failing to meet their goals – my first stop is consistency – what the hell are you doing? Why? And have you done it daily for a long period? Ten times out of ten, they have an excuse for failed consistency.

Accountability – Before I became an entrepreneur, I thought I knew what accountability was. You probably think you do too. A weekly check-in with the coach. A friend or family member asks you whether you've done what you said you were going to do. That is not the kind of accountability that an entrepreneur must garner for success.

Accountability that breeds entrepreneurial success requires daily attention and It must be measurable. To ensure long-lasting, repeatable, and replenishing success, accountability must be embraced.

Let's take a look at five simple steps. START WITH SOMETHING IMPORTANT because when this works it will spur you to new heights.

Step One: Establish an important goal.

Step Two: Structure how to accomplish the goal.

Step Three: Most important action to the structure – Determine the one thing that is necessary for the structure to stand and the goal to be reached.

Step Four: Reduce it to a set of actions that lead to a measurable outcome that can be done daily, weekly, monthly, or annually – schedule the action and do it.

Step Five: Create a log for accountability and record your progress and your setbacks – Summarize it so you know if you are making progress and what the progress is.

Stay teachable, coachable, trainable, and collaborative – keep growing.

Teresa Mack is CEO of Pacific Playa Realty, attorney, former CPA and a Real Estate broker. She manages the largest Black-owned real estate brokerage on the West Coast with over a billion dollars in closed sales volume. Co-creator of real estate sales curriculum PROPEL, she has educated/coached thousands of industry entrepreneurs.

Five of Spades

5♠ Natalie McQueen

Life Hack Your Legacy

It took a near-death experience on vacation with family to influence my passion for creating the life hack that I now teach. I never want others to feel as unprepared to leave this world as I did that day. This experience opened my eyes significantly. We have only one life to live. We never know when our time is up, so we should intentionally create and live our lives to the fullest.

Unfortunately, too many people die with regrets from self-limiting choices, not taking time for meaningful relationships, delaying life experiences, and accepting mediocrity instead of creating greatness and purpose. My life hack for creating and living a fulfilled life, then leaving a legacy is a well-planned and executed Legacy List.

What is a Legacy List, you ask?

A Legacy List is something you invest time doing, document everything you would like to experience and achieve over your lifetime. A Legacy List pulls in a more profound sense of your life's purpose and how you want to be remembered at the end of your life. So, you may have beautiful adventures, trips, and experiences in your list with specific goals and timelines for achievement, but work on the traits, skills and build the relationships you prefer over the course of your life.

What do you want your legacy to say about you? What do you want to pass on to future generations? Your legacy is how you live your life, how you make people feel, and how you impact your family, community, and the world. So, it is worth taking time now, no matter what stage of life you are in.

Sadly, research indicates that only about one percent of the world's population is living their life's purpose entirely. The research inspired me to create the Legacy Blueprint. It helps people to eliminate the things that don't serve them, target what is holding them back, and add activities to create a more enjoyable life.

Before creating your Legacy List, consider how the following steps can bring you more contentment, help you discover your purpose, and help analyze if you are really living your life or just stuck on the hamster wheel of life. First, conduct a full Legacy Life Assessment, looking at the many areas of your life impacting your state of happiness.

Then document which areas of your life you want to change. Add in things to experience more happiness, improve relationships, and reflect to find your sense of purpose. Minimal changes in one or two areas can make a big difference, or you may choose to do a complete overhaul in some places!

Work towards your desired changes daily! It is easy to slip back into that comfort zone and accept your mediocre existence. Your life may be okay, or even good, but wouldn't you prefer GREAT?

My motto is "Don't Leave a Mess. Leave a Legacy!" Creating, living, and leaving your legacy should be an exciting time. So, if you are stuck in implementing your legacy list, feel free to reach out to me, and I would love to help you Live Your Best Legacy!

Natalie McQueen is the Founder of Gifts of Legacy, an International Best-selling Author, Publisher, and International Book Launch Specialist.

Natalie has created a system that empowers families to pass on their memories, love, and wisdom through heart-felt messages within Legacy books, anthologies, and memoirs.

Don't leave a mess. Leave a Legacy!

Four of Spades

4♠ Heather Harris

The Courage to Trust, Vulnerability to Be Seen

Success means different things to different people. What does success mean to you? My dream is to be able to work from anywhere in the world I choose, make enough money to support myself and my family and spend as much time as I choose with my family and those most important to me. For me, success is all about family, being myself and having the courage to be seen. The journey to success starts with loving myself and knowing that I am enough.

I have stood in the way of my own success most of my life by refusing to be seen, holding myself small, minimizing my accomplishments and over-analyzing everything. When I failed to value myself, I found that others failed to value me too. I was telling the world how to treat me the way I treated myself. I did not appreciate or love myself. I had spent so much of my life trying to be how I thought I needed to be to fit in and belong that I lost sight of myself and forgot who I was.

What changed? What brought me out of the dark and into the light? The courage to trust, to be vulnerable and be seen. Choosing to unconditionally trust my best friend, Macario Gallegos, Jr., is the decision that changed my life for the better. Thinking back as to why I decided to trust him, it was purely intuition. This was one of the first times I trusted myself and did not get stuck in my head over analyzing. Macario has always believed in me. He encouraged me to become an entrepreneur and saw greatness in me when I did not. I am the woman I am today because of the things Macario brings out in me. I have no idea how he does it.

We all need someone in our life like this, someone we can be honest to and show our true self, who accepts us as we are and brings out our best. It only takes one person to make a positive difference. Every person I help to heal and every life I transform is a ripple effect of the positive difference Macario has made not only in my life, but in the lives of my two sons. I feel very grateful and blessed that Macario came into my life.

What pivotal moment or decision transformed your life and contributed to the person you are today? How many lives will you choose to make a difference in? Who will you choose to believe in and encourage to shine? If each of us chose to make a positive difference in at least one life, imagine how great the ripple effect will be. Imagine how much happier and healthier people in general will be. One person can make a positive difference. It all starts with you and me. Together we can help heal the world and make it a better place.

Heather Eileen Harris is an Intuitive, Visionary, Thought Leader, Holistic Wellness Coach, Holy Fire Karuna Reiki Master/Teacher, Yoga Teacher, Author, and Writer skilled at inspiring individuals to look past the barriers and challenges in life to the possibilities that exist and beyond. She is a mom, best friend, dog lover, cancer survivor and nurse who uses her experiences and knowledge to motivate and encourage greatness in others.

Three of Spades

3♠ Sharon Sills

Get It POPin!

As a successful custom balloon designer new to the balloon industry, I had to learn what it meant to start, grow, and scale a business in a lane that is not well known. There is only so much you can learn from YouTube and social media when you do not have a direct connection to a leader, teacher, or mentor.

When I first started creating custom balloons in October 2020, I didn't realize what I was embarking on would turn into a lucrative business impacting and influencing thousands. By posting my balloon setup videos on social media, I quickly grabbed the attention of clients interested in my services. Soon other balloon enthusiasts were interested in learning custom balloon design. Those individuals compelled me to start facilitating classes, but what was most valuable to them was my business advice and mentorship. In the beginning, I was unprepared for all that was included in leadership of this magnitude. Because I was so passionate about this industry, I dedicated myself to learning all that I could in every aspect of the business to help others. To date, we have trained and mentored well over 1k creatives from across the globe.

"You can have results or excuses. Not both"
-Arnold Schwarzenegger

When that voice in your head guides you to start a new business or create a new platform, there are fundamental steps that must be taken to achieve maximum success. What I learned in my journey are three pivotal things that help me master the next level of my business: WHY, WHO and WHAT. Why am I doing this? Who am I doing this for and what does my audience get out of it? This became what I am known for as an authority and expert in my industry.

Identifying your WHY. Your WHY must be big! It must be impactful, unshakeable, and goal driven. Your WHY is the reason you started your business. Your WHY will help you stay focused when challenges arise, and when money isn't flowing like the guru's said it would, and when your clients are ghosting you.

Identifying your WHO. Your WHO is imperative to the growth of your business. You must identify WHO you serve as your ideal client. This will keep you focused on where you put your efforts. Everyone is not your client so creating a WHO will focus your money, mind, and motivation on your ideal clients.

Identifying your WHAT. Your client wants to know WHAT is in it for them. WHAT products or services do you offer that will solve their problem? WHAT results do you want to gain in your business? Ask yourself, "WHAT does it look like to scale your business to the next level?"

As a business professional, the journey in life and business is intricately connected. Defining the Who, What, and Why is the secret sauce that will catapult you to the When and Where. I challenge you to make this process part of your business plan for success.

Multi-Business Award Winner and recipient of the 2022 NAACP *Up and Coming Business Award*, Professional Speaker & Author, **Sharon Sills** brings a 5-Star energetic and creative vibe to her platform.

With hundreds of professional events to her credit, she has trained and mentored over 1k Entrepreneurs from across the globe.

Two of Spades

2♠ Darryl Clack

Success Hacks for a Stress-Free Life

The assumption that the life of a professional football player is all sunshine and rainbows is far from the truth. The good times for athletes are accompanied by depression, anxiety, anger, loneliness, and stress that endures even after retirement.

Although my career as a pro athlete was amazing, it was cut short because of injuries. When my football career ended, it left me uncertain about my future. I went through a severe episode of depression and extreme stress.

As I embarked on a new journey, I had to work harder off the field to perform at the same level as on the field, causing my stress level to rise.

It's important to note that starting over is a major life decision that can trigger a variety of emotions and thoughts – uncertainty, fear, excitement, hope, doubt, regret, and freedom.

However, the crucial element that is often ignored is the state of one's mind. Stress will dominate unless you confront it. Stress consumed me. I found it tough to concentrate and anxiety made me snap at people. I experienced impatience, weight gain, poor sleep, fatigue, and headaches.

Here are 10 hacks I stand by to help manage my stress:

1. Breathing exercises: Deep breathing exercises can help calm the body and mind and reduce stress levels. Inhale for four counts, hold for four counts and exhale for eight counts.

2. Visualization: Use visualization techniques to imagine yourself performing at your best, which can help reduce anxiety and boost confidence.

3. Positive self-talk: Use positive self-talk to help boost your confidence and reduce stress levels. Encouraging phrases like, "I've got this!" or, "I can do this!" can help you stay motivated and focused.

4. Write three things you are grateful for daily. When you focus on blessings, you shift your attention away from negative thoughts and instead cultivate a more positive outlook on life.

5. Volunteer with organizations that interest you. Volunteering gives you a sense of purpose and meaning, which can help counteract feelings of anxiety.

6. Exercise. Any amount of exercise can be beneficial for reducing stress. It releases endorphins that boost your mood and provide energy.

7. Simplify your life by eliminating clutter. This creates a more organized and peaceful environment that can promote relaxation and productivity.

8. Book a flight to your favorite city. A getaway can provide an opportunity to relax and recharge. By taking a break from work or other responsibilities, you can focus on self-care and engage in activities that you enjoy.

9. Make a playlist and listen to your creation while zoning out. Listening to music can be a positive distraction from negative thoughts and feelings, which can help reduce stress.

Incorporating these stress relievers into your daily routine can improve your overall well-being and lead to greater success in your personal and professional life. However, it's important to note that these stress hacks are not one-size-fits-all solutions, and you may need to experiment with different techniques to find what works best for you.

Darryl Clack is a former NFL running back and kick returner for the Dallas Cowboys and also won the Grey Cup championship playing for Toronto Argonauts in CFL.

He was inducted into the Colorado High School and Colorado Springs Hall of Fame. He made history in 1983 by becoming the first freshman to lead Arizona State University in rushing in 30 years. Darryl achieved All PAC 10 honors and an honorable mention ALL AMERICAN in 1984 and was named ASU's football MVP.

With 15-plus years in management, he is the owner of SportMetric and has a B.A. in Kinesiology and an M.A. in Organizational Management.

DIAMONDS

Diamonds represent warmth, light, femininity. In the Tarot, they symbolize earthly matter, money, courage, and energy, but fortune-tellers often associate diamonds with spitefulness and annoyance.

~ www.fleurdelis.com/symbols

Ace of Diamonds

A♦ Maggie Bellevue

Diamond in the Rough

"Your winning card is the Ace of Diamonds.
Play it to live your best life ever."
- Maggie Bellevue

The diamond is the most highly coveted gemstone in the world, its *brilliance* and *sparkle* making it unsurpassed as a gem. Diamonds are found in clustered deposits in the Earth's crust, about 75 miles deep below the surface of the Earth.

In many respects, there is a diamond in each one of us. Our human flaws remind us just how symbolic we are of the laboratory of life. One in which our learning experiments mold our character to that fine point of refinement at which our personality sparkles with the seductive brilliance of a well-cut diamond. This stirringly beautiful expression of the interface between our *flaws* and *diamonds* also speaks to the famous cliché, *"Diamonds are a girl's best friend."*

The fairer sex cannot be blamed for this exercise in vanity. Diamonds are captivatingly exquisite. In truth, like diamonds, we were originally designed to be faultlessly and aesthetically perfect. Somewhere in our evolution, we missed the mark. But, like diamonds, we can refine and mold our character to a fine point of refinement. In other words, you are a *diamond in the rough* that is only waiting to be *cut* and *polished* into the best carat version of yourself.

To gain access to diamond deposits, prospectors have to dig deep into the ground. You are no more different from diamonds. There is a living well deep inside you, from which a river of living water flows into all aspects of your life. As you dig deeper, you will discover this treasure of your own *soul.* As soon as you discover this treasure, this *Ace of Diamonds*, you have also discovered your purpose here on Earth.

That purpose is also a *flame of passion* that has the potential to light up all your latent reserves, and give you renewed capacity for growth. That flame of passion cannot be easily extinguished, even in the face of the most daunting of obstacles.

That is the sort of passion that should consume your every waking hour. But you cannot ignite this flame unless you dream, and then insist on flying on the wings of that dream. *When you start to dream the life, you will start to live your dreams.* Our world, in the post-pandemic era, is in dire need of passion-driven *change makers* like yourself, who will pioneer a new paradigm shift with which this generation will navigate an already traumatized world.

The only way you can be such an agent of change is by ***identifying your strengths,*** and then ***positioning yourself to bring incomparable value as a solution-finder*** to any of the multiplicity of problems currently besetting humanity. Therein lies your incontestable value as an *Ace of Diamonds* in today's world.

Maggie Bellevue, 'The Apostle of Purpose,' is a Christian minister and transformational leader who, through her Treasures International (Non-Profit Organization) is a major force for transformation. She is author of the book**,** "TREASURES OF THE SOUL - *Unearthing God's Purpose For Your Life."*

King of Diamonds

K♦ Chad C. Betz

Leaving Your Assigned Hamster Wheel

Are you working towards your goals or people's expectations?

From childhood, we are guided by authority figures who keep us from burning ourselves or falling down the stairs. Today, are they guiding you away from your goals to protect you from failure?

People encourage you to have a "good job", and social media pushes money and fame as measures of success. On the surface, it looks like success. Looking deeper, a good job, money, and fame are tools to achieve success. You can run into trouble when you project these expectations onto your definition of success. You end up working hard toward other people's goals, running in circles, and never accomplishing your own goals.

To find true success, you need to determine what success means to you personally.

Identifying your definition of success is a process. If the people around you have influenced you, it can take time to unravel their expectations and identify your goals.

There are actions you can take right now to start the process of establishing your definition of success.

1. Perform an honest self-assessment – Are you:
   a. On the right track
   b. Aimlessly wandering, hoping for success
   c. On the wrong track
2. Determine how you got here – Are you:
   a. Exclusively following others
   b. Trying to succeed without a thought process
   c. Pursuing a balanced process

When you understand what you are pursuing and how you got there, consider what YOU want to do.

When I went through the process, I used the 20 goals exercise.

1. Write down 20 goals that you would like to accomplish. Your list should include goals you would consider practical but also the goals you would consider crazy and everything in between. Crazy goals are those you're interested in but never thought you could achieve.
2. After writing down these 20 goals, prioritize them by the ones you would like most to achieve. Even if you think the goal is crazy, give it a higher priority if you want to do it.
3. Look at your highest priority goals and look for patterns. What themes do you see in your goals: more leisure

time, starting a business, career change? That theme is the pattern that shows your definition of success. When you identify patterns, your highest priority goals show you the path that can lead you toward success.

When I completed this exercise, I found that most of my goals were related to writing and teaching. One of my crazy goals was to write a book. It is not so crazy now! I've written two and am working on my third. I spend more time writing and giving presentations and feel much more satisfied with my life.

Staying on the hamster wheel will lead to frustration, lack of control, discouragement, and anger. Once you understand what success means to you, you can take control of your success, leave your assigned hamster wheel behind, and achieve a success you only imagined.

Chad C. Betz is a financial services executive with over 30 years of experience, a keynote speaker, and the author of "The Second Mouse Gets The Cheese!" and "Late Bloomer, It's not too late to succeed!". He advises CEOs and coaches business-people. Chad holds a master's degree in Economics.

Chad is also a martial artist with black belts in two nontraditional styles and is currently studying Goju Ryu.

He is a husband and father of two, plus an overweight, prematurely gray dog that reminds him of himself.

Queen of Diamonds

Q♦ Diana "Dinky" Smith

Survive or Thrive?

From a country pumpkin as a child to a new life in the city starting her freshman high school year, she has come a long way. Dinky has always had just one real coach in her life, God. Their conversations have led her through many of her battles in her world.

She learned to fight the many Goliaths that came her way and never quit. She had two little girls to teach how to climb mountains and weather storms while smiling all the way. Together with heads held high, they learned how to live and enjoy their world.

After getting her real estate license in 2002, she enjoyed the fruits of her beloved industry. On her birthday in 2011, a drunk driver tragically killed Dinky's youngest daughter. The world was turned upside down and the wrong side out.

Nothing would ever be the same, life just does that sometimes. She turned her back on God because she felt he had done that to her. She became bitter and toxic to everyone around her. It took almost seven years to understand her pain and loss, grief and depression got the best of her, and she lost. This was not how she imagined her life would evolve.

Her daughter left behind a twelve-year-old child that needed love and guidance as well as a place to call home. Her father passed away when she was only eight years old. Dinky and her husband stepped up to take care of her daughter's child.

Dinky's home became her prison as she seldom left to venture into the world. Her world was her work as a realtor and raising a child. Every effort was made to do the right thing, but her mental well-being was in danger.

Dinky's oldest daughter said to her, "Mom, don't you see me anymore?" She couldn't see her only remaining child as she was blinded by pain from her loss. What could she do? She had to make things right but how could that happen at this point?

The bookstore provided much-needed material for discovery. The DSM-5 had every known mental illness and Dinky thought she had them all. Digging deeper into mental health, she found a new mission. After she found her way to recovery. With some guidance and research, she found her new assignment. She and God reconnected, and she has found a greater inner peace in her heart and life.

It took a few years for Dinky to believe in herself again and she has come a long way. Real estate is still a great gig in Colorado for her. She is authoring books on grief and depression. Her podcast is focused on mental wellness. Dinky speaks about holding IT together when life gets tough.

Life is not about survival; it is about loving who or what is in your life. To thrive is to see, feel, touch, hear, and smell the big, beautiful world you live in every day.

Own your journey.
-Dinky Smith

Grief doesn't always have trauma,
but trauma always has grief.
-David Kessler

Diana "Dinky" Smith is a Colorado Realtor, published author and speaker. After losing an adult child in 2011, Dinky's goal is to share her story of strength to overcome long-term grief and depression. Her phenomenal comeback is a great story of resilience.

Jack of Diamonds

J♦ Michael Wader

The Jack of Diamonds had a gem up his sleeve that gained him success as a leader of teams for 37 years. He discovered the diamond in a difficult way, but the experience and rewards were worth the effort.

Jack was a terrible micro-manager. He hated his workers and they hated him. He never cared about anyone and focused only on his team's production. Then one day, he was thrown into a life-changing situation.

A worker was in his dormitory room with a sawed-off shotgun threatening suicide. Jack had no training or experience in this situation, but his boss pushed him into the room with the disturbed individual and locked the door behind him. Jack did not know what to do, so he sat there quietly and listened to why the person had no reason to live.

He listened intently and empathized with the individual. Eventually, the situation was defused and turned out okay. On that day, Jack realized why his workers hated him – Jack never cared about anyone but himself and the production. That was the first day he felt he needed to care about people working for him.

The next day, a Senior leader gave Jack a book by Zig Ziglar titled, *See You at the Top*. Jack was intrigued by the book's central message: ***You can have everything in life you want, if you will just help others get what they want.*** He knew he needed to incorporate this into his leadership style. Jack developed his own slogan to remind himself of this message and repeated it over and over, sinking it deep into his subconscious mind. Then he began to live it – ***If you take care of the people, the people will take care of the process.***

Jack had never taken any time to really know the people who worked for him. He was an extreme micro-manager, but now things had to change.

Jack began asking his workers about their personal goals during annual reviews. He focused on what the workers needed to do a good job. Jack got new tools to replace their old broken ones, provided a safer workplace, and solved logistics problems that constantly plagued the workers. He focused on the needs of the workers and stopped being a micro-manager.

Performance increased, morale improved, and Jack got suggestions from the workers on how to improve processes and they implemented them together. The workers no longer hated Jack; instead, they wanted to keep him as their leader.

The hidden gem, the diamond that Jack needed to be an award-winning leader, was there for his taking, and he used it every day after that. He became an example for other leaders and shared his slogan with the younger leaders who would follow him – ***"If you take care of the people, the people will take care of the process."*** I know this story is true because I am Jack.

Michael Wader is the President and Founder of Leadership Excellence International. He is a Leadership, Lean Technology, and Active Aging trainer and keynote speaker. Michael is known as the "Inspirational Catalyst" who provides a strong call for action for his international audiences in 18 countries in the last 25 years.

Ten of Diamonds

10♦ Dr. Rhonda Glover Reese

The National Association of Shoulda Woulda Coulda (NASWC) membership is comprised of millions of people. This organization encourages mediocre behavior and thrives on it. It's mediocrity at its finest. It blocks progress and keeps you stagnant and small. This organization breeds laziness and thoughts of defeat. The members display a lack of commitment and follow-through and allow rejection to hold them back. Members tend to accept their mediocre actions and chalk it up to the fact that they can't do any better. The atmosphere is full of regret, fear, and complacency.

The members are young and old. Within the NASWC the level of education varies among the members. This organization is very diverse and does not discriminate. The social-economic status of its members varies as well. The organization is active and is looking for new members. Recruiters are friends, family, coworkers, and people on the street who actively discourage you and pour negative comments into your very being. They intend to hold you back from your destiny based on their experiences and how THEY view the world.

The dues to joining this organization are time wasted, negative words spoken, and maintaining negative thoughts. It is time invested in matters that do not stretch you nor invest in your future. This organization has three levels of membership: Sub-sociate Membership, Static Membership, and Existing Membership. Sub-sociate members don't recognize their worth and are easily distracted to go in another direction. Static members are in constant flux because they know what they are supposed to do but fail to execute their plans and create excuses. To acquire Existing membership, your language is consistently negative and lacks substance. Regardless of membership level, all members run away from opportunities screaming at the top of their lungs. They fail to recognize the importance of opportunities and are easily swayed from their destiny.

While some organizations hold annual conferences, the NASWC holds conferences daily. At a NASWC conference, members at the different membership levels are in workshops during the conference...workshops on how misery loves company and how being lazy is another form of relaxation. There are conversations in the conference hallways about how learning wastes time because everything is stacked against you. There are no conference activities to build relationships. There are no celebratory banquets where awards are distributed. If there were, members would be worried about what was on the menu and not care about the substance of the event.

There is a cost to extricate yourself from the organization. The cost is setting goals, changing negative behavior, gaining a supportive network, and being intentional about remaining physically and mentally hungry to shift and achieve a career that will allow you to leave a blueprint for success. Doing all that will get you kicked out of the organization.

By now, I hope that while this is a fictitious organization, the outcomes of it are clear. It represents where millions of people find themselves regularly. If you want to succeed in all you do, you must be intentional about staying clear of the NASWC.

Rhonda Glover Reese, Ed.D. is a 34-year veteran of the FBI, having served in various leadership roles. She is now the CEO of the Rhonda M. Glover Group LLC, a coaching/mentoring firm focusing on the development of law enforcement leaders. She is also an international speaker/trainer on leadership and professional development.

Nine of Diamonds

9♦ Dayna Caddell

As an entrepreneur who owns and operates a boutique design firm, a good part of my job is to solve problems and address the needs of my clients. However, there are a host of other factors one must implement to achieve success in business. With that said, here are some strategies entrepreneurs can adopt to keep a fresh perspective and stay at the top of their game.

It's important to stay on trend, however, one must cultivate their own style. Push yourself to find inspiration outside of your field by exploring other industries such as fashion, music, literature, and frequently, nature. Don't be afraid to examine practices such as psychology, sociology, and behavioral science. Ultimately delving into these areas of study will allow you to communicate better with clients and employees, becoming more empathetic when problems arise.

Always challenge yourself beyond your boundaries. Comfort zones only result in stale productivity. Experiment with unconventional materials and stay abreast on current software and innovative technologies to keep your work fresh and exciting.

Attend workshops and conferences with the intent to expand your knowledge and network. Swapping ideas with other professionals fosters growth through constructive criticism and cost-effective learning opportunities.

Never doubt the power of collaboration. A meeting of the minds can often be the catalyst needed to get your creative juices flowing. Also, joining industry associations is an obvious way to stay in constant contact with like-minded individuals. However, I'd encourage kicking it up a notch by thinking outside of the box. Many great ideas have been birthed from joining forces with those of diverse backgrounds, opening you up to different perspectives, that are sure to spark innovative ideas with cutting-edge results.

Though many have a love-hate relationship with it, social media can be quite useful, when its power is used for good. Connecting with influencers could very well be the inspiration needed to elevate your thought process and influence your ability to create fresh content. With that said, engagement through eye-opening content will help to build an online community, positioning you and your business at the forefront of its industry.

Guest blogging is another way to create opportunities for partnerships and collaborations and is most beneficial in staying relevant as a leader in your field. The advantages are numerous, i.e., increased visibility, exposure, and potential clients, by tapping into platforms with existing audiences that are sure to expand your reach and further validate your credibility and reputation as an industry expert.

Most importantly, stay mindful and present. Being mindful and truly engaging in the details of a project, cutting off outside distractions, allows for deeper insight and a heightened sense of creativity. Take a walk on the beach, practice visualization, and do whatever is necessary to clear your mind and cultivate fresh perspectives.

These practices encourage a well-rounded approach, that is sure to broaden the skill set of any entrepreneur, resulting in cutting-edge practice and overall success.

Multi-talented entrepreneur, **Dayna Caddell** excels in interior design and music.

Her company Dayna Caddell Design has serviced several notables and entities such as Will and Jada Pinkett Smith, record executive Jon "Big Jon" Platt, We TV's Mary Mary, TV One's Meet the Campbell's, and various Hollywood recording studios.

Dayna received a Grammy® and Dove nomination for her songwriting and has collaborated with multi-award-winning artists and producers as a recording artist.

Driven by music, architecture, fashion, nature, and a relentless pursuit of perfection, she seamlessly fuses each project into a symphony.

Eight of Diamonds

8♦ Octavia E. Vance

One of the hardest things about being a Sexologist is the stigma that seems to come with it from the Social Media world. If they're not removing your posts, stopping your ability to post for a time, or blocking your videos, no matter how tame, they're banning your entire account no matter how hard you've worked to build it. So, one thing to remember is that in this field, the road has never been void of resistance. Simply because the road of least resistance just doesn't exist in this field. You're either in it for the long haul or not. No exceptions, no in-betweens. But even in all of that, you can have success in fields where there is much resistance, especially when you truly understand what success actually is.

Many tend to think success is on the other side of resistance and that we finally obtain success once that book is published or once it's sold or once that first podcast episode is completed and edited or once that podcast is uploaded to the world to show you've done the work. No, that's just the manifestation of success. Success is actually when the idea hits you and you decide to commit to seeing it through. Because once you commit to seeing your idea through, hell or high water is coming whether it be a hacked account you've built for a decade that you can no longer access and was your main source of income or a banned account of over 100,000 followers with the income potential of hundreds of thousands if not millions, or continuously being denied a seat at the table even though you have the numbers to show you actually belong there. It's that decision to commit to seeing your idea through that determined your success years ago before the manifestation of it.

So, if there's one success hack I can give anyone, it's this valuable insight: while success is undeniably defined as 'the accomplishment of an aim, goal, or a desired purpose,' it's crucial to understand that the accomplishment of that goal is simply a direct manifestation of your unwavering commitment to see it through. Even when 'unwavering' meant pauses, delays, frustrations, and temporary setbacks, seeing it through till its manifestation, mirrors the success you first had when you committed to the process.

Remember, what you commit to, you will see through. Be Encouraged on your journey.

Your Favorite Sexologist empowers high-achieving women to embrace their sexuality and create their dream 'Ships n SexLife', without compromising their faith. With 5 books authored, 200K followers, and 4M video views, **Octavia Vance** leads in sexual liberation for women of faith. She resides in Texas with her husband and their 5 children.

Seven of Diamonds

7♦ Dawna Campbell

While teaching a class on the subconscious money mind, I asked my clients to describe a successful person. They all gave answers that were uplifting and positive. When I asked them to describe a rich person, I was shocked. I received answers that were about greed and unscrupulous behavior. The problem with this subconscious programming is, if you want to be rich, you can't be successful.

If rich people were not successful in their endeavors, they would never have the money richness. Being rich is a result of success. The key is to earn money ethically.

Successfully rich people see opportunities, potential growth, focus on rewards, expect to succeed, have confidence in their abilities, are creative, take risks, and most importantly, take action. These are all important qualities that many of my clients ask for when reprogramming the subconscious for success and why they are able to increase their money and abundance quickly.

Here are three success principles to riches, and when programmed positively into the subconscious, you become unstoppable.

Success Principle #1: The Ability to be Trusted

Trust is a key to opening doors of prosperity. With a desire for success and to magnify wealth, being trusted and demonstrating trustworthiness are a must. This is the same for your brand. Your brand needs to be trusted for quality and to deliver what it promises in the advertising and marketing. Being successful is also trusting the process that the lifestyle and wealth that you desire is possible to gain. If there is a lack of trust, success isn't possible.

Success Principle #2: Be Committed to Creating Wealth

Commitment starts with you. If you are not committed to creating your own wealth, nobody else will be committed either. Being completely dedicated to your success is absolutely necessary to creating wealth and riches. Keeping your commitments, showing up for your obligations, and taking clear decisive action results in the integrity of your business and brand. Look at your commitment level with all the areas of your life – including your health, relationships, and wealth. If there is not commitment in one area, chances are there isn't commitment to creating success.

Success Principle #3: Promote your Own Value

Successful people promote themselves and the value they offer with passion and enthusiasm. They share their value, their vision, their ideas, and their commitments. Successful people are fearless when communicating their value, bringing tremendous benefits to everyone to grow and excel. Success, riches, and wealth are the result of sharing value and makes the world a better place.

If you are not where you want to be financially or creating the success that you desire, then it is time to take action and transform old programming into creating the abundant lifestyle that you deserve.

Dawna Campbell is known as The Mind Whisperer. She is transforming the lives of Heart Centered Business Owners and Entrepreneurs creating instantaneous change while increasing your revenue 25% or more consistently. Her personal heart centered healing philosophy is to create a world that is a better place for all to live.

Six of Diamonds

6♦ Wanda Muir Oliver

Throughout my years as an educator, I learned many lessons along the way, with many of them unexpectedly coming from students. As most educators can attest, working with children requires a certain set of skills that allow for connection and effective communication. It's the connection and communication that builds trust, and they combine to create the foundation on which everything else is built. With that said, it's not much different when interacting with adults. Build a connection, communicate effectively, and build trust.

I recall a time when I was working with a group of 5 and 6-year-old students that reinforced the need for and value of a trusting relationship. We were having a discussion in which I asked them to engage in an age-appropriate discussion about emotions and their feelings. I provided names and definitions of various emotions and feelings, such as happy, sad, angry, and surprised. I also provided pictures that helped them relate to each emotion.

During the discussion on happiness, I asked for some examples. One girl described how she could tell when her mother was happy. Her example concerned the cleanliness of her room. Her mom was happy when she followed directions and cleaned her room. Students continued to share their examples of happiness. As they did, I began to think about how similar young people are to adults. We all have the same types of emotions and feelings and express them in similar ways. When things happen that we like, we are happy.

Whether young or old, we all experience what is called a dopamine response that creates, among other things, happiness. Dopamine plays a complex role in creating feelings of happiness by interacting with various brain regions and systems. While it is often associated with pleasure and reward, its influence on happiness is more nuanced. Here's how dopamine contributes to feelings of happiness:

Reward and Pleasure: Dopamine is released in response to rewarding stimuli, whether they are external (such as tasty food or social interactions) or internal (such as achieving a personal goal). This release of dopamine creates a sense of pleasure and reinforces behaviors associated with the reward. For example, when you engage in enjoyable activities like eating your favorite meal or receiving positive feedback, dopamine is released, leading to a pleasurable sensation that contributes to feelings of happiness.

Emotion Regulation: Dopamine interacts with other neurotransmitters and brain systems to influence mood and regulate emotion. Adequate dopamine levels are associated with improved mood, reduced stress, and an overall sense of contentment. Dopamine's role in regulating emotional responses contributes to a more stable and positive emotional state, which is closely related to feelings of happiness.

It's important to note that while dopamine is a significant contributor to happiness, it is just one part of a complex network of neurotransmitters and brain processes that shape our emotional experiences. Moreover, individual differences, life circumstances, and other factors also play a substantial role in determining an individual's overall sense of happiness.

How are you creating a dopamine response that increases happiness in your life?

I can share that one of the easiest ways to do so is SMILING!

When you smile you trigger a dopamine response that can also influence others and increase the likelihood of them smiling, which in turn triggers a dopamine response. It can easily become contagious!

So, whether you are young or old, <u>SMILE</u> more!

Wanda Muir Oliver is an American Poet, author of *Realities of Life*^{TM}, poetry, and short stories with a foreword by Dorothy I Height. Wanda is a contributing author to three other books and is currently working on two books to be released in 2023/2024. She has appeared in numerous plays and as an extra in a film documentary "Multitude of Mercies" featuring Malcolm Jamal Warner shown on BET International Aids Day! As an activist for change, Wanda's *Realities of Life*^{TM} touches on many areas of change, race, love, spirituality, disappointments, mentorship, leadership, and more.

Five of Diamonds

5♦ Vicki Wright-Hamilton

Throughout my journey, I have discovered key principles that have driven my personal and professional success. Today, I would like to share them, not as infallible truths but as the lessons that have shaped my perspective and directed my path in life and business.

Firstly, the principle of resilience, a lesson drawn from the early days of my career and my fight against racial and gender biases. I learned to persevere, persist and push back against the narratives that sought to box me in. I came to understand that resilience is not merely about withstanding challenges, but learning, growing, and emerging stronger from them.

Secondly, the power of adaptability became evident to me during the period of pregnancy, marriage, and career growth. Change, often thought of as daunting, became a regular feature of my life. It taught me to be flexible and to respond to life's surprises with grace and agility. It was about making strategic decisions that considered my personal growth, my family's well-being, and my career advancement.

Thirdly, I found immense value in open communication and emotional intelligence. My relationship with my husband, John, underscored the importance of these aspects. It was essential to create safe spaces for authentic conversations, acknowledge our insecurities, and seek professional help when needed. Emotional intelligence allowed me to empathize, understand, and navigate through interpersonal dynamics at home and in the workplace.

Fourthly, never underestimate the power of faith and hope. During my complicated pregnancy, the birth of my son Arthur, and an after-death experience, faith became my anchor. It instilled hope, and a positive outlook, and deepened my resolve to survive and thrive. It further revealed my purpose to me, a vision from God, to uplift others who had been marginalized.

Lastly, the ability to negotiate is a crucial skill. As a businesswoman and a mother, I used my negotiation skills to advocate for my health, my child, and my business. This helped me to exert control over situations that seemed initially beyond my grasp. To conclude, every chapter of our lives is a lesson waiting to be grasped, a story waiting to be told. Resilience, adaptability, communication, faith, and negotiation have been the pillars of my success. They have navigated me through tumultuous waters and guided me toward fulfilling my purpose. These principles have defined my journey, a journey of conquering biases, birthing life, and nurturing a successful career. This is the wisdom I've acquired on my journey. I hope these insights will be useful for your own.

My best tip for entrepreneurs striving for success:

My best tip for entrepreneurs is to master cost-cutting without compromising quality. Begin with an eagle-eyed audit of operations, evaluating expenditures. Don't overlook the power of negotiation for significant savings. Embrace technology and automation to save time and focus on strategic planning. Cross-training can build a versatile, adaptable team. Remember, cost-cutting is an ongoing process that influences decision-making, leading to an efficient and optimized culture. This dynamic approach to cost-cutting ensures sustainable growth and business success.

Vicki Wright-Hamilton is a transformative Business Acceleration Coach, Change Management Strategist & Executive Coach, passionately guiding clients towards strategic clarity and operational excellence. An empowering mentor, dynamic keynote speaker, and innovative problem solver, Vicki is committed to unlocking potential and igniting business growth, leading to both personal and professional triumphs.

Four of Diamonds

4♦ Pearl Chiarenza

Growing up, I was always eager to please others. I would go out of my way to accommodate everyone, putting their needs before mine. This people-pleasing attitude started to take a toll on my life, leaving me feeling drained, overwhelmed, and unfulfilled. But then, I decided to take control of my life and put myself first. It wasn't an easy journey, but it was a transformational one.

The first step I took towards my journey to put myself first was to learn to say "No" to others and "Yes" to myself. It wasn't easy at first, but I realized it was crucial for my own well-being. Once I was able to release the burden of pleasing everyone else, I needed to take steps to help me say "No" when needed. That's when I produced a simple yet effective life hack - placing a pebble in my pocket that I had to move three times when saying "No" to something or someone. This practice helped me be more intentional with my time and energy, and I started to prioritize the things that filled my cup.

As I continued my journey, I noticed a significant change in my life. I went from an entrepreneurial mom to a CEO Mom, running my home like a business, ensuring that everyone understood the reasons for releasing myself from overwhelm. I started to say "Yes" to the things that mattered most to me, becoming more intentional about my relationships and responsibilities. In addition, I opened the door for someone who might have wanted to be involved in a project, but before, I would have just taken on the task alone.

Now, I am proud to say that I am a SHERO of my life. I am a strong, happy, empowered, radiant, and original version of myself. My journey was not an easy one, but it was a transformational one. I learned that taking care of myself was not selfish, but a necessary step towards living a fulfilled life, prioritizing self-care in all areas of my life, including my health, emotional wellbeing, and relationships.

In 2022, we lost our son Matt at 25 and the pain was unimaginable and challenged my core. The trauma of losing Matt shook my world and left me unsure of how to continue being the strong and empowered version of myself that I had worked so hard to become. But through the pain and grief, I found the strength to stand firm in who I had become and continue to put myself first, honoring Matt's memory by living my life to the fullest.

If you find yourself struggling to put yourself first, I encourage you to act today. Start by taking the free self-care survey at pearlssurvey.com. It's a simple yet powerful tool helping you assess where you are in your self-care journey providing insights on where to start. Remember, it's never too late to become the best version of yourself. Take that first step today and unleash your inner SHERO.

Pearl Chiarenza is a Naturopathic Mental Fitness Life Coach, published author, and speaker. Her passion is helping women overcome being a people pleaser by putting themselves first guiltlessly. Empowering women to reach for more out of life so that they don't look back wondering where they were in their autobiography enables the women to become SHERO's of their lives.

Three of Diamonds

3♦ Deidra Moore

Success hacks for life or business

Let me share with you a concise overview of my personal journey, filled with significant lessons and valuable insights that can benefit others. I have this quote I share with people: "***As a child, I had no voice. As a young adult, I grew into my voice. And, now at 50 +, I've learned to listen to my voice – and trust it!***"

You see, in my early years, I faced challenges that left me feeling voiceless, unable to express myself confidently. However, as I transitioned into young adulthood, a profound transformation occurred, allowing me to nurture and assert my own voice. Now at the age of 50 and beyond, I have gained the wisdom to not only embrace my voice but also to trust it wholeheartedly.

Throughout this transformative process, I encountered various challenges and made mistakes, even going against my better judgment at times. However, I discovered profound solace and inspiration in the words of the late Maya Angelou, who wisely advised, 'Do the best you can until you know better.

Then when you know better, do better.' This powerful quote granted me the gift of self-compassion, enabling me to grant myself grace and continue on a path of continuous growth and improvement.

My experience served as a testament to the resilience of the human spirit, offering valuable insights for others embarking on their own journeys of self-realization and empowerment. I've come to understand the immense power and significance of listening to one's inner voice, which equips us with the clarity and purpose needed to navigate life's complexities.

As a mother of two, a devoted wife, a seasoned entrepreneur, an advocate for social change, a published author of three books, and a practicing attorney with over two decades of litigation experience, my voyage of self-discovery led me to discover and nurture my unique voice. Today, I wield this voice as a potent instrument to drive positive change in the lives of those open to embracing transformation. My mission is to uplift and empower all who resonate with my message.

Though my journey has been punctuated with struggles and hardships, I firmly believe that the pursuit has been entirely worthwhile. On the other side of those challenges lies something truly remarkable – my voice – an unwavering force that continues to drive me forward and inspire others to embrace change and make a profound difference in their lives.

Deidra R. Moore is a dedicated attorney and author. After leaving her job at TIAA-CREF in 1996, she pursued law school and later became a Public Defender. In 2004, she founded The Law Offices of Deidra R. Moore, P.C., specializing in Matrimonial, Mental Hygiene, Trusts, Estates, and Wrongful Death cases. Her work is shaped by over 20 years of experience. In June 2022, she published "From Me, To You," a powerful exploration of African American storytelling and generational wealth.

Two of Diamonds

2♦ Lisa Bischoff

The Past Does Not Determine the Future

Anything is possible. The past does not determine the future; I am living proof. I deserve years in prison, but I am living an abundant life that I could never have imagined.

I wrote my first software program in the third grade. I started college at the age of 14 and earned a degree in electrical engineering. A hallmark of my life is a drive towards excellence. I wanted the perfect life with all the frills.

I was willing to do whatever it took to achieve this. At age 27, I found myself drowning in over a million dollars of debt. I tried to find an easy way out and turned to crime. I was arrested for a range of offenses including computer hacking, identity theft, and theft. With these felonies on my record and the attention of the media, I was not hirable as an engineer and not even able to volunteer at most organizations. Someone marked as a thief is not someone people want around.

I sought help from a psychotherapist and clinical psychologist and was convinced I was better. I found a job and thought I was back on track. But the pattern was not broken. I slipped back into familiar ways and found myself again in debt. I relapsed back into crime, this time stealing over $600,000 in diamonds and jewelry from a client. This was my third strike.

Arrested again in September 2019, I was convinced my life was over. But God intervened. I was referred to a Christian ministry where God changed my heart and transformed my life. God showed me the root of what drove me to the destructive actions. I no longer had a desire for all the things of the world that I had been chasing. As soon as my focus changed from the things of this world to God, my life changed. Where focus goes, energy flows.

The 12-year prison sentence I was facing turned into two weeks in jail. There I saw miracles happen. Currently, I have the privilege of volunteering at the ministry that helped me. It is true that the secret to living is giving; each day I have the opportunity to help others receive healing and freedom. As a result, I continue to receive more healing and freedom in my own life. I appreciate life so much; I experience an abundance of joy. I am in the best shape of my life spiritually, mentally, and physically.

My messy past was redeemed by God. He literally continues to save my life and show me the next steps. My life story proves that anything is possible and that the past does not determine the future.

Lisa Bischoff is a Colorado Springs native with a degree in electrical engineering. Currently, she serves in full-time Christian ministry, counseling, teaching, and training people in receiving healing and freedom. Lisa loves to share her amazing testimony and is writing her first book.

UNEARTH GOD'S PURPOSE FOR YOUR LIFE
TREASURES OF THE Soul
UNEARTHING GOD'S PURPOSE FOR YOUR LIFE
DAILY DEVOTIONAL COMPANION TO
DAILY PURPOSE JOURNAL COMPANION TO
DAILY AFFIRMATIONS & PRAYERS COMPANION TO
THE APOSTLE OF PURPOSE
Maggie Bellevue
Www.MaggieBellevue.com

Teresa Rand Consulting

Award-Winning Author
Deidra R. Moore-Janvier, Esq.

In June 2022, Deidra authored, *From Me, To You: The Power of Storytelling and its Inherent Generational Wealth - An African American Story*.

Through stories about family, faith, and the power of multigenerational unity, *From Me, To You* explores the legacy of slavery in America from the viewpoint of enslaved Africans and their descendants. Deidra proves that African American history is American history and that these two concepts rely on each other for posterity.

In September 2022, *From Me, To You* made its debut as a resource in independent schools, in NY State. Moreover, in October 2022, after an extensive vetting and selection process, From Me, To You, is now on bookshelves throughout the New York Public Libraries. It can be part of your library of book by going to Amazon for purchase.

In August 2023, Deidra was recognized with an award from the National Association of Black Journalists for her book and work within the African American community.

Made in USA - North Chelmsford, MA
23704_9781648102417
10.27.2023 0519